Five Minutes to Orgasm Every Time You Make Love

Cover design by Somberg Design, Ann Arbor, MI

Five Minutes to Orgasm Every Time You Make Love

Female Orgasm Made Simple

2nd Edition Revised

Five Minutes to Orgasm Every Time You Make Love

Female Orgasm Made Simple

D. CLAIRE HUTCHINS

JPS Publishing Company
Grand Prairie, Texas

Five Minutes to Orgasm Every Time You Make Love
By D. Claire Hutchins

ISBN 0-7394-1278-7

Permissions

Excerpts from *The Hite Report on Male Sexuality* by Shere Hite, © 1978 by Shere Hite, Reprinted by permission of Alfred A. Knopf, a Division of Random House, Inc.

Excerpts from *With Pleasure: Thoughts of the Nature of Human Sexuality*,© 1995 by Paul R. Abramson and Steven D. Pinkerton, Reprinted by permission of Oxford University Press, Inc.

Excerpts from *Woman: An Intimate Geography*, ©1999 by Natalie Angier, Reprinted by permission of Houghton Mifflin Company, All rights reserved.

Excerpts from *The Technology of Orgasm: "Hysteria," the Vibrator, and Women's Sexual Satisfaction*, ©1999 by Rachel P. Maines, The Johns Hopkins University Press

Contents

Five Minutes to Orgasm Every Time You Make Love
By D. Claire Hutchins

Foreword

It might have started with Clint Eastwood. There he was, slow-dancing with Meryl Streep in *The Bridges of Madison County*, looking deep into her eyes, even sharing a bubble bath. Women were convinced that if tough-guy Eastwood could make a lady's day with endless foreplay, then maybe her Dirty Harry could too.

As a writer who deals with men's health issues, I have attempted to understand how women define their roles in healthy sexual relationships. Sometimes it's not so easy. "It was the most romantic, careful, drawn-out sex I'd ever had," reads a highlighted confession in a top woman's magazine. And in another, there's this recipe for the perfect romantic weekend: "Fill the house with flowers, dance together in front of a fire, kiss and cuddle -- but don't have sex until the end of the weekend."

Come on gals! Must great sex be preceded by a timeless tease?

Think for a minute about all the prerequisites you place on sex. Do you shower beforehand, brush your teeth, slip into something more comfortable, dim the lights, make sure the kids are asleep, lock the door, pull the shades and ready the birth control? It's like some NASA countdown. Then if all systems are finally go, comes the act itself--the kissing, the touching, the positioning and all the other sequenced bedroom behavior leading to a successful mission. Unfortunately, any one of a hundred preliminary checks can signal trouble and postpone blast off -- especially for women. Too often you get left behind in the mad rush to ecstasy.

Most expert advice in the field of sexual compatibility is given to mood-setting and sensitivity. But this is contrary to nature. "Humans were designed for fast sex," says J. Dudley Chapman, M.D., Ph.D., a gynecologist and sex therapist for 25 years. "The animal kingdom wasn't used to wasting time. The more time you spent cohabiting, the more vulnerable you were to being consumed."

To take this evolutionary stuff a step further, you could argue that such a sexual waltz may even be detrimental to the species. Indeed, more men than ever are seeking professional help for performance anxieties and premature ejaculation problems. It seems men know how to have sex, but we aren't so sure about how to make love. And it's tearing many men apart.

"There's a lot of sexual anxiety in men," says Dr. Chapman. "Did I do right by her? Will she be mad at me afterward?" It's not that men are intimidated by romance. It's just that they're not sure how much, how far or even when.

"Performance anxiety runs rampant among the men I see," agrees Michael Seiler, Ph.D., a certified sex therapist with the Phoenix Institute in Chicago. "Men are struggling with issues of sexual desire. They're often confused about their own right to assert themselves sexually."

Instead of putting the pressure on men to slow down their sexual response time, can women be taught to speed up?

Women have a physical hurdle to overcome. While the penis is directly stimulated during the typical sex act, the clitoris is only indirectly aroused. This doesn't mean that women are incapable of reaching orgasm quickly. In fact, according to Judy Seifer, Ph.D., R.N., President of the American Association of Sex Educators, Counselors and Therapists, both men and women can usually masturbate themselves to climax in one to two minutes.

It doesn't take much to convince men of the merit of "quickies," once considered the ultimate guy sex act. The tricky part is making the case to women, who may believe that endless foreplay is the only way they can reach climax. Now D. Claire Hutchins promises faster orgasms for women, thereby relieving men of the responsibility of bringing their partners to orgasm. Ms. Hutchins shows women that quickies can be therapeutic, in addition to just plain fun. They not only help men and women find time for the relaxing, rejuvenating flush of sex during a hectic day, but also take the pressure off men to always be the Clint Eastwood of her dreams.

Ms. Hutchins sets aside storybook seductions in favor of fast, fun, satisfying sex. Sex without music by Kenny G or flowers from FTD. With her three-step formula, you can reach orgasm as easily as a man. And in these busy days, when the alternative to a long-drawn out lovemaking session is often no sex, it can be a relationship-saver.

Joe Kita

Introduction

For Women Only

A few years ago, a poll in the *National Enquirer* found that the majority of women would rather go out to dinner than have sex. Why? There could be many reasons, but for a significant number of us, reaching orgasm is **JUST PLAIN DIFFICULT**. If it takes too long – 30 minutes, 45 minutes, or an hour – for us to reach climax, we lose interest.

"Men are like microwaves.
Women are slow cookers."

As a woman, you are slapped with the label of "Slow Cooker." Everyone from the so-called experts to the man on the street will tell you that, when it comes to the difference between the sexual responses of men and women, the time it takes men to climax generally ranges from ***fast*** to ***too fast.*** Women are **slow**, often **too slow**. Many women can't reach orgasm without extended penile thrusting, vibrators, or oral sex. Some never reach orgasm at all.

Not for Women Only

The fact that *his* rocket lifts off before *your* final countdown even begins could be classified as a **serious sexual dysfunction**. This spells problems in many good relationships. Very few couples recognize the problem, or admit it if they do. Yet the disparate timetables of many couples – she takes too long or he comes too fast, depending on your point of view – has caused unnecessary heartache, not to mention physical discomfort for both partners, but especially for YOU, the female.

It is popular to blame the man for the unsatisfactory timetable. One of the first lessons a young man learns, or tries to learn, is to slow up. The problem is not that the woman is *too slow*, it's that he's just *too fast*. Some men are premature ejaculators, but, excluding physical problems and/or the onset of impotence, you never hear of men being too slow. The vast majority of men, even up into their 70s or 80s, have orgasms quickly compared to women. You won't find a book about *coming* faster written for them.

Unlike young men, society lets women off the hook. As women, we are told there isn't anything we can do. It's out of our hands.

Scour the magazine stands, and you will find that plenty has been written on the subject of female orgasm, but women are rarely blamed for being slower to climax than men. It's not very fashionable these days to blame the woman for a couple's sexual incompatibility. The word "problem" isn't used. The agony of a too-slow, unreliable or nonexistent orgasm may leave women frustrated – but it's just a fact of life.

Women are brainwashed to feel thrilled to have any orgasm at all, no matter how long it takes.

Even though experts and even our men bend over backward to absolve women of any blame, deep down inside, women often feel disturbed with the whole setup. Absolved of blame, we may still feel deeply guilty for having given away our *responsibility*.

Female orgasm is the simplest thing in the world, yet we humans, experts and nonexperts alike, have made it hopelessly complicated and sometimes absurd. If men are tired of waiting for us to reach orgasm, we are even more tired of trying to catch up. Maybe it's not your fault.

But you sure as hell can fix it!

Why Me and Why Now?

Women are different from men, but are we that different in our sexual response? Are we really "slow cookers" while men are like "microwaves?" Like men, can we reach orgasm fast, AND every time we have sex?

I can. You can too.

I had an orgasm the first time I had sex. That orgasm by itself doesn't qualify me as an expert because my first orgasm was an ***accident!*** I couldn't repeat my success in later lovemaking experiences. And no wonder. When that first orgasm tore through me, I didn't know what it was! Of course I had heard of orgasm before, but I was totally inexperienced (except for extremely heavy petting), and until you've felt an orgasm, it is almost impossible to describe. I didn't know at first that this was an **ORGASM**. And I sure didn't understand the steps I took. (I took most of the appropriate steps without realizing it.)

The next time my lover and I had sex, I couldn't have an orgasm, but when I understood what an orgasm felt like, I was ready to go again. The feeling was so wonderful compared to anything I had ever felt before, I knew I would never be "satisfied" with sex without achieving orgasm. Later, when I couldn't duplicate my orgasm, my lover and I were ready to experiment.

Nobody told us how. I was so young and ignorant, I didn't even know where to look for information. Fortunately, my first lover and I were young and inexperienced – ready to give anything a try! We finally got it right. Through trial and error I became orgasmic again, but most of the credit goes to my boyfriend. More experienced than I, though not by much, he was a tender, skillful lover, ready to cooperate. He was good at holding back his orgasm until I had mine. Learning how to have sex was fun, but if I had to take that kind of time today – the gyrations, changing of positions, trying this, trying that – at my age now, I would be worn out!

I had to work hard to have orgasms.

A small percentage of women are supposed to have hot spots, the nipples, ears, neck or inside the knees, which, when caressed at the right time, will cause them to have an instantaneous orgasm. Some women are supposed to have orgasms if they are looked at the right way, or while giving a man oral sex. I read a story about a woman who had an orgasm while standing in a grocery store check-out line! I've *read* or *heard* about these women. In my interviews and casual conversations, I've never met one personally. But, setting aside my skepticism, I will admit that definitely does not describe me. After I replaced my first lover, my pursuit of orgasms yielded mixed results. My orgasms were unreliable at best, but occasionally a superior sex partner would "get me off."

Sometimes if it took too long to reach orgasm, I gave up and faked it instead.

Times changed. During the sexual revolution of the 1970s, I became more experienced. Women like myself now had the opportunity to explore alternatives. We became more open about sexual pleasure and how to get it. We experimented with our boyfriends, we talked, and we learned from our partners and from each other. By the 80s and 90s, I had learned to have reliable orgasms.

I found a technique that worked every time and as soon after actual sex began as I wanted.

There is absolutely no reason why women today should have difficulty reaching orgasm; yet, judging by popular literature, it seems that women are still obsessed with the subject. The technique I have mastered is by no means the **only way to have an orgasm**. Many techniques can help you become more orgasmic and some may even help you achieve orgasm faster. Anything from good communication with your partner to a healthful lifestyle can help.

But if your orgasms tend to be hit or miss or if you want them to be easier and faster . . . .

Then try my technique, what I call the ***quick and easy formula***. I am not a counselor, or a so-called "expert" in the field of female sexual response, and I didn't invent this technique. Thousands of women successfully used it before me.

Actual realization that I had a technique that worked came when my husband was dying of a brain tumor. My husband couldn't walk, and he was losing his ability to speak, but he was still having erections. A home nurse told me that we should continue to have sex for as long as possible. Even though he couldn't do much but lie on his back, I was able to give him the pleasure of sexual release AND enjoy myself.

Through my own experience and from honest and open discussions with other women, I have zeroed in on this common problem. I'll share what I know, and you will meet some of the other women (and men!) who have benefitted from the technique in this book.

You will NOT learn skillful foreplay techniques, multiple positions, or how to be a better lover.

You don't need to greet your lover wrapped in saran wrap or lacy lingerie, light candles, or take co-ed bubble baths. This is definitely NOT about pleasing HIM. There are plenty of sex manuals for that sort of thing. *Want to please your man in bed? Buy something else.*

This book is about pleasing YOU.

But first, we have to ask . . .

1

What Do Women Want?

After a period of stimulation, there is a sudden, intense sensation known as orgasm, climax or "coming." It is described in many ways: burning, explosion, vibrating, pressure and tension, all followed by intense relief. Unlike what men would like to think, women normally do not show outward physical signs like writhing and moaning. Many become completely stiff and still.

Orgasm for men is most often synonymous with ejaculation, but female orgasm is a little more difficult to pinpoint. Researchers at the University of Sheffield tested 28 adult women to measure length of time, intensity, and change in blood flow during orgasm by inserting a small electrode into each woman's vagina. Each woman indicated the beginning and end of her orgasm after masturbation. The average orgasm lasted twenty seconds, but there was no relation between how long it lasted and how intensely it rated.[1]

Not all orgasms are created equal. There are **orgasms** and then there are **ORGASMS**. Not every orgasm has to rock your world. The feeling in your genitals is extraordinary, but in a great orgasm, all body parts – breasts, anus, mouth, lips, ears, thighs, fingers, toes – among other body parts – participate. As men and women approach orgasm, the muscles of the arms, legs, back, feet, face and hands – the entire body – tightens to the point of cramping; the toes curl and the face distorts in a wild expression.

Orgasm acts as a powerful pain relief agent, and bolsters immune functioning. It relieves tension and stress. But most of all, orgasm FEELS GREAT.

Unlike eating and breathing, you won't die if you don't have an orgasm, but sexual satisfaction often colors how we view the rest of the world. What do YOU want from an orgasm? What do most women want? I think the most important requirement for an orgasm is RELIABILITY. Every sexual experience should be rewarded with orgasm. We should be able to count on orgasm every time we make love. Second, we don't want to wait all night to have one. Simply stated, it should be **EASY**, it should be **FUN**, and it should bring that feeling of **RELEASE**.

Should You or Shouldn't You?

A few centuries ago NEITHER sex was supposed to actually *enjoy* the sex act. Sex was for making children; that was it. Any other purpose for the sex act was supposed to be unnatural. Where would such an idea come from? This principle was adopted by the early Christian Church from the Romans' principle of *natural law*. *Natural law* was defined as the principle that rules all animals, and all animals are regulated by an innate understanding of this law, including humans. *Natural law* dictated the union of male and female, the procreation of children and their proper education.

Nonprocreative sex was therefore a crime against nature.

Using the principle of *natural law*, an early church leader, Saint Thomas Aquinas, argued that nature designated the ejaculation of semen to create children and perpetuate the species. If semen was expended for any reason other than reproduction, it was contrary to nature and *sinful*. Therefore, one of the worst sins was engaging in sex for the sake of pleasure, even within marriage. Four activities were particularly abhorrent: masturbation, bestiality, homosexual copulation, and heterosexual coitus in other than the Church-mandated "missionary" position.[2]

Intercourse was to be performed with as little emotion as possible.

St. Paul counseled abstinence for those who wished to remain pure. For those unable to control their animal lusts, they were advised to marry, "for it is better to marry than to burn" (1 Corinthians 7:1-9). It wasn't until the late 16th Century that the Church legitimized sexual pleasure for husbands and wives, but only if procreation remained the main purpose and no contraception was used.

In Victorian America, the last half of the 19th Century, the prevailing sexual code prohibited premarital sexual relations. Many medical and moral authorities advised that sexual intercourse be limited solely to the purpose of procreation, even in marriage. Although the idea of separating orgasm from pleasure is ludicrous, the concept of pursuing pleasure during sex did not exist at the time, or, if it was discussed at all, was linked to "lustful, bestial, and uncivilized behavior."[3]

In Western societies, the pursuit of sexual pleasure was legitimized by the sexual revolution that marked the decline of Victorianism at the turn of the Twentieth Century. Unfortunately, those great changes still left women far behind.

For most of us, these ideas are laughable today. But it wasn't that long ago when you think about it. If you are 20 years old, a century seems like a long time. If you are 50, it seems like nothing at all. What is surprising is even though these ideas seem funny today, we are still tainted by the attitudes of those earlier centuries. Especially women. *We live in a society where there is incredible sexual freedom on every level, and yet less than half of the women are consistently orgasmic.*

Are Women Entitled to Have Orgasms?

Do these centuries-old attitudes affect your willingness to change and stifle your ability to achieve the kind of orgasm you deserve?

As odd as this question may seem, there was a time when the idea that a woman was entitled to an orgasm was an unthinkable, even evil idea. Men got to "enjoy" their orgasms first. In 1809 an anonymous male author advised:

> You must first lay it down for a foundation in general that there is an inequality in the sexes, and that for the economy of the world, the men who were to be guardians and lawgivers had not only the greater share of bodily strength bestowed on them, but those also of reason and resolution. Your sex will be the better prepared from this necessary reflection for the compliance and passiveness that may be required and is necessary for the better performance of those duties which seem to be most properly assigned to it by nature.

The Female Friend; or the Duties of Christian Virgins to which is added, Advice to a Young Married Lady.[4]

Even as late as 1947, women were characterized as sexually passive. Ferdinand Lundberg and Marynia F. Farnham, in *Modern Woman: The Last Sex,* described the woman's role in the sex act as:

> It is not as easy as rolling off a log for her. It is easier. It is as easy as being the log itself.[5]

Compared to logs! Thankfully, attitudes about sexuality in women went through a revolution, but not until the late 1960s and the wide-spread use of the pill. For the first time women were not punished for being sexually inventive. It is easy to forget how different things used to be. An old movie like *Anna Karenina* shows us how "promiscuous" women ended up. Anna was shunned by society for leaving her husband for another man and threw herself under the wheels of a train and was crushed. If heroines committed adultery in old movies, they died, regardless of how viewers might sympathize with their plight.

It wasn't until the 1960s that Hollywood began to let the wayward woman survive, and by the 1970s the sexual revolution was in full swing, *giving women the right to enjoy sex for pleasure without making childbearing a requirement.* Finally, women realized that . . .

2

Sex without Orgasm is Like Kissing Your Mother

Jenny:

Not having an orgasm HURTS!

What about the woman who can't come at all during sex, even with extended thrusting, vibrators and oral sex? With all the information women have at their disposal today, it is surprising that 10% to 15% of all women report that they ***never reach orgasm at all***. Only about **half to three-quarters** of American women climax regularly during sexual intercourse, no matter what the stimulus.

Even these dismal statistics may be overstated. *Reported statistics* will never be exact because women are under pressure to appear normal and feminine in their sexual responses, and researchers often slant data. When researchers Masters and Johnson made their sex study in the 1950s, it was known that women who orgasm regularly through intercourse alone were a tiny minority, but Masters and Johnson and their followers sacrificed the objectivity of scientific thinking when they chose women for their famous study. They selected only women who regularly reached orgasm in coitus, apparently deciding that these represented normality, even though the experience of the majority usually represents the norm! It wasn't until Shere Hite attacked the Masters and Johnson results in 1976 that questions were raised about their methods of selection.[6]

Countless studies have produced little hard, reliable data. Husbands, doctors and researchers want to hear that phallic stimulation during intercourse is as satisfying for women as it is for men, so female orgasm during intercourse is often over-reported. Women have a tendency to say what their husbands and doctors want to hear. My own less-than-scientific surveys and other literature shows that the penis is not the most effective means of producing arousal and orgasm in most women.

Diane Grosskopf was commissioned by *Playgirl* to study 1,207 women and her study was published in 1983. Masturbation was shown to produce orgasm more reliably than anything else. All but a small number of the respondents said they did not feel cheated if they did not experience orgasm during sex. "Three-quarters of the women felt it more important for their partner to be pleased than for themselves to be pleased."[7]

In 1985 Ann Landers' newspaper column shocked the world by reporting the results of her inquiries to readers about how they felt about the sex act. Of the 100,000 women who responded, 72 percent wrote to say they'd rather be doing something else. In other surveys, women often rate orgasm as important, but not essential.

Is emotional satisfaction more important to women that physical orgasm? I'm sorry, I just don't buy it. When women feel free to tell the truth, especially to themselves, they admit that not having an orgasm is frustrating, at the very least.

Patty:

> *If I am very aroused, and I don't have an orgasm, I feel frustrated and inadequate for being too slow or incompetent. Physically, I feel shaken and a little sick, almost like abdominal cramps, with pain in my groin and genitals. Not having an orgasm is worse than having no sex at all.*

It is not easy for us to admit that the culturally ingrained symbol of "manhood" is not the ultimate sensual magic wand.[8]

Sex without Orgasm for Men?

You've got to be *kidding*! Orgasm-less sex is not a man's problem. Men tend to be consistently orgasmic; failure to reach orgasm is a statistical rarity. This is true for all ages, from 18 to 65 plus years. Even though the percentage of women reaching orgasm improves to about 65% as they age from their late twenties to middle age, too many women are still denied the orgasm experience.

Why should orgasm be less important for us? Are some women incapable of orgasm, or do they simply need the right stimuli or partners?

Many women have given up on any man finding the *magic button*.

Since the sexual revolution, the pill and the rise of feminism, women understand they have the right to participate in and enjoy sex on an EQUAL basis with men. Even so, many are still in pursuit of the elusive "Big O."

Why Do You Want a Quicker, Easier Orgasm?

Beth:

> *Sure, I have orgasms – when I have time. When Jim and I first met, it was a lot of fun to*

take our time playing, kissing, cuddling, and making out. Then came marriage, and day-to-day living sometimes got in the way: careers, kids, activities. We just don't find the extra time to spend on lovemaking any more. I still have orgasms all right, but not every time. Jim usually has to pump away at me for what seems like hours before I finally come. Sometimes, it's just not worth going through all of that, for him or for me.

There are many reasons we want faster orgasms. Extremely long, drawn-out lovemaking sessions are wonderful in a fledgling relationship, but after a while they can seem like too much work. Even worse, a man's continual thrusting in and out of a woman's vagina in an effort to help her reach orgasm, can actually hurt. A prolonged sexual encounter can be agony for the woman, but men don't always realize this. I've heard men brag that they can "go all night." Sometimes they wear this "skill" like a badge of honor. They don't realize that women are not sexual continuous motion machines; endless pumping can get to the point where it actually hurts.

Women can't and don't want to go on forever. No wonder the glamour quickly goes out of the marriage bed. It is not surprising that women would rather go out to dinner than have sex.

Who is to Blame?

Joyce:

> *If my husband comes before me and rolls over and goes to sleep, I feel frustrated, cheated and angry. I've heard men can be trained to satisfy women, but more often than not a good night's sleep and work the next day are more important than what I need.*

Judy:

> *It's a big letdown, and irritating to see him lying there all peaceful and satisfied.*

A woman's difficulty reaching orgasm is not just her problem. It's her partner's problem as well. If you are feeling frustrated, how must he feel?

If it takes too long for you to reach orgasm, your lover may be a little bit disgusted.

He may resent you because you take so long to have an orgasm. He feels somewhat perturbed and a whole lot frustrated. To say he's unsympathetic would be a huge understatement. Especially when, nine times out of 10, he has to do all the work. He has peaked a long time ago, and let's face it – your desirability is fading with every fruitless thrust.

Her partner's attitude can add to a woman's sexual frustration, making it even more difficult to come.

Women who can't reach orgasm and do so quickly often feel like they are too demanding, especially if they blame their partner for their failure. So sometimes we just shut up. But that doesn't really solve the problem.

Sherry:

> *Sometimes I enthusiastically fake orgasm to keep my partner from being disappointed because he couldn't stimulate me enough.*

If the woman does manage to have one or more orgasms, then it is the man's turn. His climax ends up anticlimactic. The typical sexual pattern can leave everybody tired and bored, and none too anxious to repeat the whole process.

A majority of women who masturbate do so within four minutes, a statistic that is almost identical to men's. Why then are we so much slower at reaching orgasm during intercourse?

True sexual dysfunction comes from a mix of mental and physical problems. It is not the purpose of this book to deal with deep-seated psychological and mental problems of a traumatic or neurotic nature, nor with extraordinary physical problems.

Ordinary problems – like inexperience and fear – can slow or even cheat a woman out of having an orgasm. But, the "problem" MOST of us face – women like Beth and Sherry – comes from something so simple we don't even think about it. The mismatched timetable of many sexual relationships is the physical realization of an unfortunate blend of concepts with which we have been saddled.

What we too often fail to understand as couples is that most of our problems stem from what I call . . .

3

The Sex Offenders

The Missionary Position

When Saint Thomas Aquinas and the early Christian Church declared that the one correct, **god-fearing** position for having sex was the man on top, any other sexual position was considered sinful. But, as European travelers entered exotic lands, they brought tales of how far off people did **IT** in unacceptable ways. People changed, and most people today don't conform their lives to those old teachings. Still, the missionary position is the most popular position for lovemaking. Why?

The missionary position is the worst position you can adopt to fine-tune your lovemaking.

A woman's external or visible genitals are grouped under the term *vulva*, which includes the inner and outer "lips" and the slit between them, which is the opening to the vagina. The vagina sheaths the man's penis, but there are no nerve endings within the deepest part of the vagina.

Thomas:

> *Even though my wife tells me it isn't true, I blame myself when she can't reach orgasm during intercourse. If I had a bigger penis, maybe she could climax. I guess I'm not 'man enough.'*

Men often blame themselves for a woman's failure to reach orgasm, but it isn't their fault. No matter how big a man's penis is, in the MISSIONARY POSITION, it is nowhere near the clitoris.

When it comes to orgasm, women are blessed with a small but significant "magic button."

Nerve endings comparable to a man's penis are located outside the vagina (near the top of the vertical slit) in the clitoris, a little protuberance redder than the surrounding pink membrane. The clitoris arises from the same region of the fetal genital ridge as the shaft of the penis, but is not like the penis. The clitoris does not perform "practical" functions like urination or ejaculation. It is a single unit of 8,000 nerve fibers, a higher concentration of nerves than is found in the fingertips, lips, and tongue, or anywhere else in the body, and twice the number in the penis.

> In a sense, then, a woman's little brain is bigger than a man's. All this, and to no greater end than to subserve a woman's pleasure. In the clitoris alone we see a sexual organ so pure of purpose that it needn't moonlight as a secretory or excretory device. [9]

Many women cannot touch the clitoris directly because it is almost painful. The shaft of the clitoris itself has relatively few nerves, but it contains thousands of blood vessels which allow it to swell during arousal. The base and shaft of the clitoris are mostly hidden beneath the skin of the vulva, and there is an underlying clitoral system is as large and responsive as the male penis. This includes two broad roots which become engorged with blood, a pair of caverns that fill with blood, a sponge-like structure, sets of muscles that contract rhythmically during intercourse and a network of veins throughout the pelvic area.

The total blood vessel engorgement of the clitoral system expands as much or more during arousal as a man's, but a man's engorgement (erection) is outside the body and visible. The female engorgement is not.

A scarce supply of nerve endings in the inner two-thirds of the vagina don't allow much vaginal sensation from deep penetration of the penis, and the clitoral powerhouse is three inches above the mouth of the vagina. That's why . . .

Achieving clitoral stimulation through penile thrusting is almost impossible.

Even today we have a poor understanding of female anatomy, because most of a woman's sex organs, unlike a man's, are located inside of her body.

A man's most sensitive area is the little piece of skin on the underside of the penis running from the coronal ridge, the edge of the mushroom-like top of the penis, to the penile shaft. In the missionary position, the entire penis, including this area, is buried deeply within the moist and warm vagina. During thrusting, the penis receives intense stimulation, and this results in eventual pelvic muscle contraction, orgasm and ejaculation.

In the womb we all start out with the universal X chromosome – as **women**. As the fetus develops into a male, *what would have been the female clitoris changes into a male penis, and the female labia fuse to become the male scrotum (with the tell-tale seam down the middle)*. The area under his testicles corresponds to the vagina on you.

Thrusting the male penis into the female vagina is anatomically the same thing to YOU as rubbing the scrotal skin (balls) – pulling it back and forth causing the skin on the upper tip of the penis to move – would be to HIM. Using this form of stimulation would cause a man to need MUCH longer to reach orgasm during intercourse. If all a man could do to have an orgasm was rub the spot directly under his testicles, *orgasm would be as difficult and slow as it is for you.* You, too, would have to be patient and understanding.

All female orgasms are achieved by stimulation of the clitoris and expressed by vaginal contractions. Alfred Kinsey (*The Kinsey Report*) and his associates demonstrated that **MOST**, and probably **ALL**, women ***require stimulation of the clitoris or labia to reach orgasm***. Masters and Johnson subsequently indicated that female orgasm during intercourse results not from vaginal sensitivity, but from indirect stimulation of the clitoris.

Yet the myth of female orgasm from penile thrusting persists.

In some women, the skin around the urinary opening is exceptionally sensitive, and because this tissue is pushed and pulled quite vigorously during coitus, such hypersensitivity could result in a comparatively easy orgasm through the thrustings of intercourse alone.

Some women feel they climax best with the application of pressure deep within the vagina. Named for German gynecologist Ernst Grafenberg, a small mass of tissue is called the "G" spot. The G spot is said to be a two-inch cushion of highly erogenous tissue located on the front wall of the vagina, right where the vagina wraps around the urethra, the tube that carries urine from the bladder. Hyped in the early 1980s as a revolutionary discovery, the G spot was defined as a sort of second, internalized clitoris. Allegedly, stimulation of the G spot in the missionary position brings some women to immediate climax.

Some believe that the G spot is located in the "Skene's glands," which generate mucus to help lubricate the urethral tract. Others think that it is the sphincter muscle, which keeps the urethra clamped shut until you're ready to void. Still others question its existence altogether. Why invent some magic place when the exiting structure does quite well? The roots of the clitoris are deep, and probably can be tickled through posterior agitation. In other words, the G spot may be nothing more than the back end of the clitoris.[10]

Many women felt inferior because they couldn't have an orgasm this way. Many couldn't even find it! I haven't found a G-spot, and most of the women I talked to haven't found one either.

Apparently, this discovery was not so revolutionary that it cured the problem for a significant number of women. Suffice it to say that for *most* of us, there are not two kinds of orgasms.

Regardless of how friction is applied to the clitoris, female orgasm is almost always evoked by clitoral stimulation. Clitoral stimulation can occur during sex. Rear entry sex may allow the man to reach the woman's clitoris, but only by using his fingers. If the woman lies face down, she may rub her clitoris against the bed or sheets, or even stimulate herself.

In the 1992 book *The Perfect Fit*, Edward Eichel and Philip Nobile made news by introducing another "new" position called "coital-alignment technique," or CAT, which described a method recommended by sex educators for years. It featured the man on top, his pelvis positioned higher on the woman's pelvic girdle or "riding high" on the upper vulva and pubic bone.[11] This creates an angle of the penis into the vagina that is meant to rub the clitoris when the man thrusts or when he grinds his penis in a circular motion. Not bad for some of us, but many women I interviewed found the position stiff and uncomfortable, and doesn't allow the female much movement.

Other sexual positions work for some couples, especially after a long relationship, countless adjustments, and a period of hit or miss. For many of us, they don't.

The Legacy of Sigmund Freud

Janet:

> *This is the way I manage to have an orgasm when my husband is on top. I wriggle my body underneath his as rapidly as possible, which massages my pubic area. As you can guess, it isn't too easy with him on top of me. Bill usually manages to keep from coming too soon, but just barely. It takes a while, but I usually climax.*

We can't change the fundamental difference between women and men, the way our bodies match up during sex. How then do we improve our sexual relationships other than asking men to slow up? Janet goes to a lot of trouble to get her clitoris directly stimulated. Other women may settle for the old "in and out" or pumping away, and eventually they may experience orgasm during coitus because the inner lips pull the clitoral hood with them, actually stimulating the clitoris. Although a woman may eventually reach orgasm this way, sex takes longer than it has to *because the feeling is weak compared to direct touching or rubbing in the clitoral area.*

Why keep knocking ourselves out and ending up frustrated over a technique that is so inefficient?

Having gained the freedom to experiment and the acknowledgment that women, like men, are entitled to pleasure during the sex act, women had yet another hurdle to face –

The myth of the vaginal orgasm.

Sigmund Freud, the father of psychoanalysis, believed that women who had orgasms from direct *stimulation of the clitoris only* were sexually immature, while women who had orgasms from *intercourse* were sexually mature. The transition to womanhood meant transferring sensitivity from the clitoris to the vagina. Women were sexually "anesthetic" (according to Freud) if the clitoris "stubbornly" retained this sensitivity. His theory maintained that clitoral orgasm is like masturbating, an activity Freud attributed to little girls. He insisted that the clitoral focus of young girls should yield to *vaginal dominance*, a sign of being a mature woman, like fully developed breasts. In Freud's view, a woman who did not experience pleasure primarily from vaginal intercourse rather than clitoral stimulation was fixated at a childhood stage of sexual development.

Freud popularized the theory of two kinds of female orgasm and that so-called vaginal orgasm was expected from normal adult women, but he was not the first to raise the question of where female orgasm originated. Instead, Freud's theory was a glitch in the acceptance for thousands of years by experts and amateurs that the clitoris was the center of a woman's sexual pleasure.

It was twentieth-century post-Freudian medicine, however, that elevated the vaginal orgasm to a veritable Holy Grail of sexual function for women. When Alfred Kinsey dared to question both its existence and the necessity for adjusting women's sexuality to fit an inappropriate 'norm' some of his colleagues reacted with horror and outrage. Bergler and Kroger defined frigidity as the incapacity of women to have a vaginal orgasm during intercourse. Bergler and Kroger insist that there is no scientific difficulty with arguing that 80 to 90 percent of all women are 'abnormal' and go on to defend the Freudian notion that real women are satisfied only by penetration. To give these authors their due, they are at least evenhanded about their normative illusions: they assert that 'mature, normal men do not desire sex except with women they love tenderly.'[12]

Ann:

I have no problem having an orgasm when Brian performs oral sex, but he wants me to climax when he's inside me. What's wrong with me? Why can't I have a **real** *orgasm?*

Ann and Brian are frustrated by Sigmund Freud's unfortunate legacy. The belief that you must have an orgasm *without* some form of direct stimulation of your clitoris adversely affects the lovemaking of many couples, whether they have heard of Freud and his theories or not!

Women, you can forget Freud!

Based on zero clinical evidence, Freud's theories of female sexuality are wrong in a number of ways, but it has taken about fifty years for experts and the lay public to realize how little he knew. The residual effects of Freud's ideas still influence couples like Brian and Ann. Freud's theories were just that – only theories that were never proven. You must realize, in order to have orgasms when you want to, the way you want to, that . . .

All female sexual pleasure is connected physiologically with the clitoris.

The role of the clitoris in female orgasm cannot be downgraded. The female clitoris serves the same function as the man's penis. But, unlike the penis, the **sole function of the clitoris** is the generation of pleasure. Notwithstanding Freud's theory, although by no means the only erogenous zone, the clitoris is the **one organ** specifically devoted to sexual pleasure.

But if the clitoris exists to give us pleasure, then why do we have to work much harder for our finale than men do?

Who is built wrong? Me or him?

Neither! The primary pleasure organs of men and women (his penis, your clitoris) DO NOT join or rub each other during the typical sex act performed in the missionary and most other coital positions.

Women can't alter their physiology in order to conform to what is expected of us, so we adopt countless strategies to reconcile reality with expectations, including faking orgasm. But who loses? Women do, and so do men. Instead of faking it, let's just accept our bodies and move on. Let's ***adjust***.

The debate between the clitoral verses the vaginal orgasm accomplished SOME good. It convinced women that ***orgasm does exist***, and that all women can have them without guilt. Clitoral orgasm is **guaranteed**, if you know your own body well. The same organ that guarantees your orgasm can help you have one as fast as you wish, if you . . .

4

Become a Control Freak

A number of women DO have orgasms during intercourse, but the reasons aren't mysterious. Since all orgasms are caused by direct or indirect stimulation of the clitoris, some women can achieve orgasm from penile thrusting. As the penis moves back and forth, it pulls the labia minora, which are attached to the skin covering the clitoris (the hood), indirectly moving the skin and thereby stimulating the clitoris. Most therapists and researchers agree that this is less efficient than direct clitoral stimulation, and works for only a small percentage of all women. For that percentage, it doesn't work all of the time, and certainly not very fast. Consequently, we are stuck with the label "slow cookers."

Natalie:

> *I had an orgasm the first time I had sex. And why not? My boyfriend and I had been building up to it for 5 months. (I held out so long because, back then, good girls didn't do it before marriage.) After that, reaching orgasm wasn't so easy, but my boyfriend and I were willing to experiment. Even though he wasn't a virgin, he wasn't very experienced either. We read books, looked at magazines and asked friends. I still didn't understand what made me climax the first time, so we started trying different things. We usually made love in his car, but lying down in the back seat was so uncomfortable, we finally started using a position where he sat up and I straddled him. He could use his hands to help me move up and down on his penis, and, by parting my vaginal lips, I was able to get direct clitoral stimulation from his penis. I started having orgasms again, almost every time.*

Women who experience orgasm during intercourse consciously or unconsciously attempt to center the clitoral area for maximum contact. This is the way men get stimulation as well. By "rubbing" the penis against the vaginal wall, they are receiving stimulation in the same area they stimulate during masturbation. *You must do the same thing.* Stimulation must be centered where it **FEELS GOOD**.

As you can see, Natalie's orgasm was not a result of her and her boyfriend sticking to the missionary position when it didn't work for them. Natalie was fortunate enough to discover early on what it takes many years for most of us to learn, and she had a partner who was willing to experiment. Great sex takes practice.

There is simply no position that works as well for the majority of women who want to have a ***quick and easy*** orgasm as the female-on-top position. In . . .

Step One . . .

You climb on top!

Why?

The female-on-top gives you control of the action. There isn't anything that automatically makes female-on-top work, except it gives you great freedom of movement. This position may take a little bit more work than many of us are used to, but you are ***in charge***. Too many of us make the mistake of just lying back and expecting the man to do all the work, and then wondering why we don't have the orgasm we want. Sex is a partnership. To make it truly sensational, you must take ***at least*** an equal part in the action. For you, it's exciting to be in control for a change and to know you can do anything you want.

The clitoris can't be forced. A woman who worries that she is taking too long for her partner will take that much longer.

> In my view, all the intricacies we've been mulling – the apparent fickleness and mulishness of the clitoris, its asynchronicity with male responsiveness, and the variability of its performance from one woman to the next – can be explained by making a simple assumption: that the clitoris is designed to encourage its bearer to take control of her sexuality. Yes, this idea sounds like a rank political tract, and body tissue has no party affiliation. But it can vote with its behavior, working best when you treat it right, faltering when it's abused or misunderstood. In truth, the clitoris operates at peak performance when a woman feels athunder with life and strength, when she is bellowing on top, figuratively if not literally.[13]

Have you seen the movie *Something Wild* with Melanie Griffith? How about *Basic Instinct*? The underlying message of these movies is that . . .

***Female superior* is for passionate,**
exciting, even dangerous women;
the missionary position is for WIVES.

How it Works

After you and your partner have participated in foreplay, however much you want, and when you feel ready for sex, have your man lie on his back, his penis aroused and standing ready for you to straddle him. Don't be in too much of a hurry to get him inside of you. *Take advantage of the opportunity to display your body; he will love watching you work.* With him on his back and you on your knees, swing one leg over him and balance your weight on your knees. Then lean forward to take some of your weight on your hands. Take his penis in hand and rub your moist vaginal lips and clitoris against it. Tease the head of his penis by sliding it back and forth across your vaginal opening, occasionally inserting just the tip and taking it out again. Finally, slide it in gently and slowly. You may need to use a free hand, or he can use his, to guide his penis into your vagina. Straddling his thighs, you lower yourself onto his penis. Once he is inside of you, sink down on him, remaining upright from the waist up.

In this position, **YOU** control the depth of penile penetration and the pace of thrusting. **YOU** manipulate the amount of friction and the speed. **YOU** have an infinite variety of movements. You can raise your body up and down, bend forward with your breasts touching his chest, or slide your breasts back and forth. You can move your pelvis and abdomen sideways and in all directions to give different kinds of erotic pleasure. Lean forward to create friction between his pubic bone and your clitoris. Men may want to arch their backs and raise their pelvises to help create a connection between the clitoris and penis.

Try all variations and see what stimulates you most. You will be very deeply penetrated, and the man's most sensitive area is buried deeply within your moist and warm vagina. Your partner can rest while enjoying exquisite sensations. When you have your orgasm, he can feel the rippling of your vaginal muscles much more intensely than in any other position.

Above all, this position is comfortable for most women, gives us greater freedom of movement, and puts us in control of our own orgasm. Some of us may be *mentally* uncomfortable with what our psychological inhibitions may be telling us is aggressive exhibitionism. Tell your mind to **SHUT UP**! Be sure to close your eyes, at least part of the time.

Don't examine your body, don't worry about how you look, and don't try to analyze what HE is thinking throughout the whole thing.

Burt:

When Betty and I have sex with her on top of me, I feast my eyes on her whole body displayed above me. I can watch as her vagina envelops my penis. I like to watch her beautiful breasts sway with every move. And I can reach up and play with them anytime I want. I can run my hands down her belly and over her buttocks with my hands. Most of all, I enjoy the passion reflected in her face.

By parting the vaginal lips and leaning forward to your partner's chest, you can bring your clitoris directly into contact with the base of the man's penis, and rubbing the exposed shaft of his penis against your clitoris may be all the direct stimulation of the clitoris you need to reach orgasm.

Another option is to have your lover place his thumb on your clitoris and hold it firmly in place while you move up and down, but the position of his hand may feel somewhat awkward for you both. *It seems that when men stimulate their partners, they don't do it very well.* Maybe he feels awkward, embarrassed or resentful. I believe most simply do not share the same sense of rhythm as their women. And, it is also objectionable because you've turned your response back over to him.

For some women, changing from the missionary to the female-superior position may be all that is necessary to achieve orgasm easier than you ever thought possible.

Learning how to "ride" your man will make you a champion at lovemaking.

Your control of the action and pacing of the thrusting should enhance your sexual response, but it may not be enough. Not everyone can reach orgasm this way, and even if you can, it may not be very fast. Faster than waiting for his penis to thrust you to orgasm perhaps, but still not fast enough. Grinding pubic bones or rubbing his penis against your exposed clitoris is a tricky way to reach orgasm. It requires your partner's full cooperation. A new partner's body shape or sense of rhythm can still leave you hanging. That's why I suggest that most women, especially if they want to reach orgasm reliably and **F A S T**, use STEP TWO.

By using Step Two, you will once and for all free your man from . . .

5

Slavery to the Female Orgasm

Carol:

> *I get furious if I don't have at least one orgasm. No matter how long it takes, I make Robert rub my clitoris until I have one.*

Since most women require direct stimulation to the clitoris than can be provided coitally in order to reach orgasm, does that mean that something is "wrong?"

Not unless you are a man who has been enslaved in the pursuit of the female orgasm. Men are traditionally pressured to maintain an erection and extended thrusting during intercourse in order to "give" the woman an orgasm.

> Just as the man has traditionally been considered the 'provider' economically – the man should 'bring home the bacon' or buy the house–he has also been given the role of 'providing' the woman with sexual satisfaction. A 'real man' should 'make her come.'
>
> In addition to the pressure created by this role, this idea also often puts the man in a no-win situation since the information he has been given–that thrusting during intercourse should bring a woman to orgasm–is faulty.[14]

This puts an inordinate amount of pressure on the man, possibly causing doubt about his masculinity and encouraging women to fake orgasm.

> *If anything goes wrong, I'm blamed for it. Girls always seem to just lay there and say, 'O.K., make it happen.' I feel an immense pressure to perform and feel that it's all up to me.*
>
> *I feel a little incapable not being able to make her orgasm during intercourse. I don't see*

> *how any male can go on long enough to do this.*
>
> *I felt in my marriage that there was something wrong with my performance since she didn't orgasm and I suffered greatly. It deprived me of much enjoyment and made me guilty and uncomfortable.*[15]

Men have believed they were performing like they were supposed to perform, and that women are "supposed" to orgasm from their thrusting alone. If thrusting does not provide what the woman wants and needs, men have felt uncomfortable, frustrated and guilty. Many feel (mistakenly) they have failed because of the size of their penis.

What we women and our lovers go through to get our sexual needs met! Considered "helpmates" in a male-dominated society, women have been afraid to stimulate themselves during sex with men. "Being dependent on men, economically, socially, and politically, has kept women silent."[16] Instead of torturing ourselves with "why don't I orgasm easily during intercourse," we should want to know why anyone still ridiculously demands that women have an orgasm from penile thrusting that doesn't involve clitoral stimulation.

Direct stimulation from thrusting his penis during intercourse makes reaching an orgasm easy for the man. ***All we need is the same thing*** – direct stimulation of the pleasure organ – his penis, our clitoris. Women have tried everything they can to reach orgasm with sex, and failing that, have resorted to oral sex and vibrators for stimulation of their clitoris. When this happens we can reach orgasm, even have multiple orgasms, easily!

Jo:

> *I've never had an orgasm through intercourse alone. All of mine have been through oral sex. If my partner hasn't found the right spot, I am not afraid to show him. If the pressure is not right, I tell him.*

Oral Sex

Oral sex is a popular and growing practice, but only about one-third of men continue until the woman reaches orgasm. Most men consider it foreplay, not sex. Is it the best answer to the problem of the disparate sexual natures of men and women? Even though half of all men state that their sex partner's pleasure is more important than their own, and are willing to perform cunnilingus on their partners until they reach orgasm, there are some men who do not enjoy performing oral sex, and even though they rarely (VERY RARELY) complain about being on the receiving end, there are others who ABSOLUTELY refuse to do it. Why not?

Some can't deal with pubic hair. They find the natural look unattractive or they may fear ending up with a mouthful of hair. Others find the natural aroma of a woman unpleasant. Some feel subservient, and they prefer to feel dominant.

Fran:

> *Usually I am confident and outspoken, but when it came to asking a new partner to perform oral sex —my 'sure thing' in terms of orgasm, it gets difficult. What if he doesn't like it? What if he thinks I am selfish? I speak up and then cringe because I usually sound like an instruction manual. My last boyfriend didn't act like he really enjoyed giving me oral sex (though he loved being on the receiving end!).*

Men have borne responsibility for women's sexuality; Caprio told young husbands in 1952 that "the sexual awakening of the wife was their responsibility."[17] Her failure equals his failure. Consequently, some men enjoy giving oral sex, but some just want to please their partners and don't enjoy it very much.

Shere Hite reports

> ...[T]hat many men saw fit to stress [cleanliness and smell] with regard to women's vulvas seems to reflect the influence of the age-old patriarchal view of female sexuality (and women) as being 'dirty,' 'nasty,' or 'not quite nice.' Each child still learns this in the story of Adam

> and Eve; it was Eve's sexuality and 'desire for carnal knowledge' which ruined the Garden of Eden and for which men and women are still being punished – especially women, who are told that they must henceforth bring forth children in pain and suffering.
>
> The vulva, of which women are taught to be ashamed (the medical term for the vulva is 'pudendum,' a Latin word meaning 'of which one ought to be ashamed'), has been hidden away for so long that few people really know what it looks like. The general impression many men have is of a dark wet place, with an unfamiliar smell, a kind of unknown space into which the penis ventures courageously.[18]

I have little sympathy for men who find oral sex "unpleasant." You may be able to coax a reluctant lover to perform oral sex by shaving or by using a scented douche (not often, as douching is unhealthy). Improving your diet by eating more fresh fruits and vegetables can improve all body aromas, so go for it – if you want to.[19]

Many men don't mind performing oral sex on their partners, and most actually enjoy it – now and then. ***Unfortunately, oral sex requires a lot of work on the man's part.***

Ron:

> *I love oral sex, and I love the way it makes Suzanne feel. But sometimes I'm just too tired to get into sex that much. And I don't understand why oral sex has to be the whole thing. I mean, it's okay as foreplay, but my lips and tongue can get tired after awhile. And she sure doesn't do the same thing for me. If she had to perform fellatio on me every time I wanted to have an orgasm, she'd probably leave me.*

Guys like Ron are often afraid to admit they don't enjoy oral sex that much. They are afraid of being inadequate lovers, anti-feminist, selfish and hung up.

Darla:

> *When my husband decides that his method of stimulating me – usually oral sex – is not working fast enough, he changes without asking me. I end up feeling frustrated, angry and sad.*

Oral sex makes women inactive participants in the sex act – worked on – like our partner is just performing a job with our orgasm as his paycheck.

Is it fair to call oral sex a problem? Not unless one or both partners don't enjoy it.

Vibrators

Soon after train travel became a common method of travel in the nineteenth century, it was much debated over whether it was good or bad for women, primarily because it subjected them to vibration.[20]

These days, a vibrator is fast, easy, and efficient.

In her very funny and educational book, *The Technology of Orgasm*, author Rachel Maines gives an account of how the vibrator first emerged as an electromechanical medical instrument. While researching another subject, Maines found advertisements in women's magazines that dated back to 1906 for equipment that strongly resembled the devices now sold to women as masturbation aids. Her interest was piqued, and future research yielded an interesting history. The electromechanical vibrator, it seems, was invented in the 1880s by a British physician to be used by physicians to treat women diagnosed as "hysterical."

Surprisingly, from the time of Hippocrates until the 1920s, massaging "hysterical" female patients to orgasm was an ordinary medical practice among Western physicians. Hysteria was then a common illness in women and was diagnosed as a lack of sexual satisfaction with symptoms of chronic arousal: anxiety, sleeplessness, irritability, nervousness, erotic fantasy, sensations of heaviness in the abdomen, lower pelvic edema, vaginal lubrication, flushing of the skin, voluptuous sensations, embarrassment, and ***confusion after recovery from a very brief loss of control - usually less than a minute.***

Since physicians did not enjoy applying pelvic massage and considered it a chore, the vibrator was invented to implement the efficiency of a mechanical device. The vibrator performed therapeutic massage that didn't tire the therapist.

> In the first two decades of the 20th century, the vibrator began to be marketed as a home appliance through advertising in such periodicals as *Needlecraft, Home Needlework Journal, Modern Women, Hearst's, McClure's, Woman's Home Companion,* and *Modern Priscilla* mainly to women as a health and relaxation aid, in ambiguous phrases such as 'all the pleasures of youth ... will throb within you.' When marketed to men, vibrators were recommended as gifts for women that would benefit the male givers by restoring 'bright eyes and pink cheeks' to their female consorts. A variety of models were available at all price ranges and with various types of power, including electricity, foot pedal, and water. An especially versatile vibrator line was illustrated in the Sears, Roebuck and Company *Electrical Goods* catalog for 1918. Here an advertisement headed 'Aid That Every Woman Appreciates'

> shows a vibrator attachment for a home motor that also drove attachments for churning, mixing, beating, grinding, buffing, and operating a fan.'[21]

Doctors relieved hysterical women of their symptoms with manual genital massage until the women reached orgasm, but orgasm was a forbidden subject, so it was clinically defined as "hysterical paroxysm." Medical authorities, Maines writes, were able to justify the clinical production of orgasm in women as necessary to maintain the dominant view of sexuality. Sex was penetration to male orgasm – a practice that, then and now, denies orgasm to a majority of the female population. Such treatments were socially and ethically permissible for doctors, but not for the women themselves, and women's sexuality was considered a disease requiring treatment.[22]

Since a great number of women were diagnosed as hysterics before the middle of this century, but the diagnosis finally disappeared, it suggests that perception of the behavior has altered, not the behavior itself.

Female orgasm should be simple, but for many it has become a chore. Husbands and lovers have taken the place of physicians in manipulating the female to orgasm. I have no objection to oral sex and vibrators at all – unless they are *always* used as a replacement for the sex act and *if* partners think they have no other choice. Orgasm through cunnilingus and vibrators is fulfilling, at least for the recipient. ***But the man's penis is not inside you, and you are not having intercourse.***

The popular syndicated radio personality, Howard Stern, shared on his morning show how he felt about his wife's vibrator. When they had sex, he claimed, he used it on her before she could achieve orgasm. He typically complained that she started to take longer to reach orgasm even with the vibrator. He resented the extra work. He complained that she was getting a callous "down there."

Although research indicates that some women find a vibrator enjoyable, some find it painful, annoying and distracting. While it can be an occasional source of fun and variety, when it becomes an expediter to bring a woman to orgasm quickly and save time, problems may result.

Only the most determined of romantics could find this scenario exciting day after day, year after year.

Make Me Come!

The man on top, thrusting and pumping for hours, oral sex, vibrators, rubbing her clitoris until his hand and shoulders ache; is there anything wrong in all of this? Is the *answer* to the neglect of female orgasm that men should learn to give better clitoral stimulation? I don't believe it is, in spite of the "expert" advice you see in most magazines – "tell him what you need and want in bed."

A man's orgasm usually does not depend on the skillfulness of his lover, the timing, or any kind of genital manipulation by his partner. A man has control over his own orgasm, moving and thrusting in ways that are best for him. If his partner performs genital manipulation or oral sex on him, that's a bonus to the pleasure of the sex act, but most likely, he will reach orgasm anyway.

Sometimes women are encouraged to be lazy.

By insisting on oral sex or vibrators, women seem to expect the man to be in charge. He must orchestrate the seduction, arouse his partner and keep himself from coming too soon. In the old days, women waited for men to lead sexually, to make initiating moves. Females were passive. *We have moved from the days where women were supposed to feel no pleasure at all, even revulsion over the sex act, to later times when women were allowed to feel pleasure, but only as passive recipients of male lust.*

Today, female orgasm is often *the* goal in sexual encounters. We are supposed to be that way – we are told by most sexual "experts." Nowadays, we are advised to depend on the man to *give* us an orgasm, as if a female's orgasm were a gift that a male could bestow! If we allow men to control our orgasms, are we really that far removed from the role of the passive female?

What happened to women's liberation?

Today, men must postpone their orgasm long enough to awaken the female to pleasure. A *real* man today must be a mechanic, manipulating a woman's sexuality through clever stimulation, self-control, timing, endurance and even the patience to wait for her to experience multiple orgasms. An adept lover can only pretend to be romantic; he has too many jobs to perform during sex to really feel that way.

A woman may expect a man to spend as much as 20 minutes on oral sex or 30 minutes using a vibrator on her so that she can reach orgasm. Let's admit the truth. That's a lot more work than we would be willing to spend on them.

When we turn our orgasms over to any lover, skillful or not, we put responsibility for orgasm back on the man, dependent once again.

Caren:

> *Until a year ago, I was involved with Joe, with whom I always made fabulous love. Without Joe, I don't feel comfortable or familiar with my body. Since our breakup, I've gone to bed with some wonderful men, but no one has yet helped me explode with such wild intensity. I'm not sure exactly what Joe did to me, he just seemed to have those magic hands.*

Caren could be waiting until the next century for another man with "magic hands" to show up, or she could begin exploring how her body responds to various levels of clitoral stimulation. She'll soon discover exactly how Joe touched her and won't have to wait for a new partner to hit her "magic button." She can freely use the same technique herself.

Please do not misunderstand me. I am not opposed to oral sex, vibrators, mutual masturbation or anything else that gives satisfaction to both partners in the sex act. Outside stimuli can be fun. What does concern me is the excessive reliance women have upon something other than themselves, especially something that depends on their PARTNER's performance. If men can control their own orgasm, why must this be wrong for women? As infants we had to lean on someone, to be dependent. Some dependency is normal, for men and women, but women are encouraged to be dependent to an unhealthy degree. We women are taught that our orgasms are out of our hands, literally.

If we have a lousy lover, we are out of luck.
No orgasm. Better luck next time.

Who's in Charge Here?

There used to be no choice; all women were supposed to be passive. Things have changed. Women who control their own economic lives have choices. **We may lead, control, and be aggressive.**

Ellen:

> *I've never climaxed with a man. I get very little out of intercourse any more, even though I used to enjoy the kissing, hugging and cuddling as much as I enjoyed the sex act itself. I can masturbate myself to orgasm easily and often do, but men seem to move too fast to let me begin feeling what I feel during masturbation.*

Women think they must choose between intercourse OR clitoral stimulation by masturbation when alone, oral sex or vibrators. Why not consider self-stimulation during coital sex as a possibility? If you are an adept masturbator, why wait until you are alone to have an orgasm? **During sex, the man's penis filing your vagina, you can have your orgasm through direct stimulation of the clitoris.**

Barring deep-rooted psychological or physical problems, you can easily have an orgasm every time you make love. All it takes is the willingness to adopt a technique that helps you achieve orgasm any time, at any pace, on YOUR timetable. Oral sex, vibrators, or any other method your lover uses to "make" you come, can be replaced when you masturbate yourself during sex. If you have lost hope that a man can find the magic button and know what to do with it when he does, remember there is someone who can go right to it and know immediately what to do – YOU. A skillful, clever lover is always desirable to both sexes, but not necessary. As a woman, you do not have to wait on men to initiate and control sexual activity. You already know how to achieve orgasm through self-manipulation. ***Use it during the sex act with a man.***

Do we really need men? Why not masturbate alone? To many women, the full penetration of a penis seems to enhance the orgasm by filling the vagina, and will more than likely intensify your orgasmic pleasure, more than when you masturbate alone. But happiness, sexual or otherwise, rarely depends on someone else – nor should it. Women fought hard for equality. Unfortunately, it seems that, in bed at least, we are often advised to turn right back around and give equality – in the form of control of our orgasms – back to men.

The wish to be rescued goes back to the days of cave living when a man's greater physical strength was needed to protect mothers and children. But allowing the man to induce your orgasm, and thereby give up control, is no longer appropriate or constructive.

If you learn nothing else from this information, I hope you have learned to THINK ABOUT YOURSELF, your desires, wants and needs during the sex act.

Orgasm is essentially a selfish act. This is something that men have realized for years.

Andrea:

> *My mother was 34 years old when my father died. She was uneducated, had two daughters to support, and there wasn't very much insurance money. Totally unprepared, she had to find a way to support herself and my sister and me. It wasn't only money either. She had to learn to change a tire, manage a budget, and make household repairs that my daddy used to make.*
>
> *Consequently, unlike many women who grew up with a father and/or brothers, I grew up very independent. Today, I don't rely on a man to support me, financially or emotionally. A man is nice to have around, but I sure don't wait on him to MAKE ME COME.*

Reassume your responsibility. Sex based on subordination, with one person giving pleasure so the other person's is enhanced, whether it be a man OR a woman, is exploitative. Men should not expect to bring a woman to orgasm on demand, and a woman should not escape her sexual responsibility. Women must take responsibility for at least HALF of the sexual experience, and quit making our partners virtual slaves to the female orgasm.

You have the ability and the responsibility to participate as a technically proficient sexual equal with your partner.

Use it. Learn from women who are successfully orgasmic. Without a doubt, a great majority of them can say . . .

6

I Get By with a Little Help from My Hand

The best way to learn to orgasm is to masturbate.

Want to speed up your sexual response? More than any other activity, masturbation is the MOST important activity to quicken your orgasm.

Maybe you already know how to masturbate by yourself. If so, great. If you don't masturbate or are not proficient at it, don't let the idea of masturbation frighten you away from adopting this method. People used to believe that masturbation caused blindness in men.

Female masturbation simply did not exist; it wasn't spoken of until recent years. Masturbation finally came out of the closet in 1972 when the American Medical Association declared masturbation to be "normal."[23] Today, two thirds of all men ***and women*** see masturbation as a natural part of life. If you don't masturbate or have never tried it, you owe it to yourself to give it a try.

Kelli:

> *When I was growing up, no one I knew admitted to masturbation or discussed it. It wasn't condemned. It wasn't even discussed. When a boyfriend gave me my first pornographic book to read, I had my first conscious sexual fantasy. I was turned on; masturbation was my relief. I worked at it awhile before I found release, which was quite a trick since I had to use a stall in the dorm bathroom. My boyfriend was surprised when I told him I had masturbated for the first time.*

Once again, we can learn from men. They have traditionally masturbated far more than women. Boys usually begin masturbating at an early age and often masturbate to orgasm during adolescence. They are encouraged to learn about their bodies, their world, and taking risks in general.

Women of every age are less likely to masturbate than men, and feelings of guilt often affect their ability

to reach orgasm, according to *Sex in America*, a widely publicized study conducted by the National Opinion Research Center. Little girls are generally given less freedom to explore their own bodies and those of their friends because they are more closely supervised and discouraged from exploration – of themselves or outside themselves. Adults watch them more closely, discourage any kind of risk-taking, and protect girls more than boys. Boys are encouraged to explore, take risks and get dirty.

Like Kelli, many women did not learn about their bodies until they began having sexual encounters with men. The subject of masturbation, especially learning how to masturbate, is still an explosive subject. Surgeon General Joycelyn Elders, a President Clinton appointee, was fired when she suggested at an international AIDS conference that children should be taught masturbation in sex education classes as a way of preventing unwanted pregnancies.

Maybe she was right.
Learning how to masturbate is really a great idea.

Studies show that failure to orgasm is **five times higher** among women who never masturbated than among the rest of women. Out of approximately 10% who never orgasm, 95% have also **NEVER MASTURBATED**.

Now that's a statistic that can be changed.

Learning how to masturbate is a way to know and understand your body, how it reacts to definite physical stimuli, and how to have an orgasm, especially if you have never had one. Even if you are older, it isn't too late. Masturbation is *very* important for the woman who never played with her own genitals as a young girl.

Through masturbating yourself, you will learn the difference between the clitoris, labia, urethra, and vagina. Masturbation will help you become more orgasmic and a better sexual partner. It will enable you to assume responsibility for your share of the sex act, more capable of giving and receiving pleasure. For many people, the emotional and physical release decreases tension and irritability. It is one of life's greatest sources of sexual pleasure, a thrilling release from tension, and a beauty treatment that will keep you glowing.

Masturbation Can Be Fun!

Most of you already know how to masturbate. If you don't have the necessary practice manipulating your genitals, I have included some instructions. There are many books, magazines and videos that can help you out. A large number of the magazines devoted to women contain articles about masturbation. Many will also have advertisements for information as explicit as you wish to get.

Gina:

> *I was 15 years old before I realized my vagina was a separate opening from the urethra. That was partly my mother's fault because Mom told me, in a well-intentioned effort to talk about sex with her young daughter, that the man put his thing into the place where she makes pee-pee and that makes babies. Hey, that's better than not being told at all, isn't it? At least she was in the right vicinity. I finally located my vagina by learning to use tampons.*

If you are totally unfamiliar with your body, squat over a mirror and inspect your genitalia. Begin by exploring the outer lips, your clitoris, urethra, and vaginal opening; notice their size, color, and relative positions.

Begin by lying on your back with easy access to your genitals. Think only pleasant thoughts. Massage your breasts, massaging them in circles with your palm; rub the nipples -- they will become erect and hard. In most women, the nerves in the breasts are connected to the sex organs, and you will increase the sensation in the genital area.

Slowly insert a clean forefinger into your vagina. Circle your finger to touch the walls of your vagina, touch the rough end of the passageway at the cervix. Squeeze your vaginal muscles and see how it feels. A man's penis feels the same sucking feeling. Remove your finger and massage your entire genital area with it. Part the genital lips and find the clitoral nub. When you hit upon this spot (it will feel very pleasant to touch, much more sensitive than the surrounding areas), begin by gently rubbing it. Rubbing around the area will probably be more pleasurable than massaging the clitoris itself, which may be too tender to massage directly. Using one finger, three fingers, or your whole hand, rub the hood of tissue that covers the clitoris firmly and gently. When aroused, you will feel the clitoris become erect. As your pleasure builds, rub faster and more insistently, back and forth or in a circle until stronger and stronger throbs of pleasure occur. Experimenting with different levels of intensity, continue this movement until you reach an orgasm.

This is the basic idea. If your body tells you to rub faster and harder, do so, but orgasm may elude you if you try too hard. If so, slow your pace, let up a bit, relax, and let your body adjust to a new pace. If you try to force an orgasm when you think you're ready, you may end up causing an unpleasant sensation instead. Relax, and start a gentle teasing again. You will have your orgasm, just don't try to force yourself. Practice masturbating until your orgasms become bigger, quicker and more reliable. Practice alone until you can bring yourself to orgasm at will.

Anna:

> *I had never actually touched myself – not consciously at least. I found it a very difficult thing to do. I wasn't bought up to think of*

> *masturbation as a sin, but it still felt wrong. Nevertheless, I overcame my inhibitions and soon learned that I had never climaxed before. Once I knew what I needed, and what a real orgasm felt like, I knew what to do with my lover or alone.*

Practice, Practice, Practice

Besides being immensely pleasurable, masturbation keeps your sex muscles in shape and is the best way to find out what really turns you on. Books and therapists may give good guidance, but you have to FEEL sexual pleasure yourself. I can't stress enough how important masturbation is to the ***quick and easy formula***. The more you learn about your sexual appetites and desires, the more you pleasure yourself, the sexier you will feel. The more practice you get, the faster at reaching orgasm you will become. Finally, you will be ready to try out your new technique with a man.

Or skip this part completely, and begin practicing your masturbation with a man.

Sherry:

> *I masturbate several times a week and have no trouble bringing myself to orgasm in minutes. I tried it during sex with a man (masturbating*

> *myself), and it worked the same way. Just as good —just as fast.*

Masturbation is essential for women to catch up with men in understanding and appreciating the sex act. You are practicing in order to improve your sexual response. Learn to masturbate whether you have experienced orgasm or not, because this is a major part of the technique you will be using during the sex act.

Masturbate in bed, on the couch, in the bathroom, anywhere you can find a few minutes to yourself.

Now any woman – YOU – can achieve orgasm, even multiple orgasms, as often as you wish. How fast? How long does it take to reach orgasm when you masturbate? Five minutes or as little as 30 seconds? According to scientific research, most women can achieve orgasm in 3 to 5 minutes, when masturbating alone. And this, mind you, is starting "cold," before fantasy or actual stimulation begins. *Imagine how much faster they could be if they were already excited by a desirable sex partner and foreplay?* These statistics are based on women who masturbate regularly. If you are slower than this average, you can improve with practice.

By using the same technique during intercourse, **by practicing manual stimulation of your clitoris *during intercourse*,** you can coax yourself to orgasm in a matter of only a few minutes.

Step Two

After foreplay, when you are "warmed up," and reasonably attracted to your sexual partner, your vagina is moist and ready. Positioning yourself on top as you learned in the previous step, you are in a comfortable, convenient position to masturbate yourself to orgasm.

Since the studies of Masters and Johnson, it has been well known that women have orgasms during sex because of clitoral stimulation, regardless of whether they are aware of the stimulation (masturbation, vibrators, or oral sex) or not (pulling and rubbing of the clitoral "hood" by the thrusting penis). **Though this knowledge is often hidden in popular wisdom, educated and sexually confident women must reject the theory that manual stimulation of the clitoris during sex is abnormal, unnecessary, or sick.**

By learning how to masturbate yourself to orgasm while your partner is penetrating you, you have the opportunity (not to mention relief) to redefine sex as intercourse that includes the orgasm of BOTH partners. Millions of women enjoy orgasm during intercourse by using additional stimulation of the clitoris. The question should not be, is this wrong? Can this be fixed? The question should be, why do we keep asking such a stupid question in the first place? Why resort to everything in the book, from scented candles and coed bubble baths, to extensive analysis and sex therapy to MAKE orgasm happen any other way?

Ladies – let's move on!

If the thought of touching yourself in front of your partner scares you, you'll have to get over it.

Why Wait?

Mastery of our sexual anatomy is the fundamental lesson of this book. Creating one's own orgasm is sexual independence; though its nice to have a skillful partner, it is important to know that it isn't necessary for orgasm to take place. Giving ourselves an orgasm is sexually the same as being able to change a flat tire or support our kids.

Self-masturbation during sex or *assisted* orgasm, as I think of it, allows you to control your orgasm response. This is the essence of achieving an orgasm quickly and easily, and something ANY woman can learn to do for herself – without turning her orgasm over to a man. We don't have to wait on men with "magic" hands, or skillful tongues.

In this fast-paced world, why should women have to wait on men to control our orgasm response? We can be ready, willing and able to do it ourselves, and still enjoy participating in the sex act with him.

A reluctance to use the ***quick and easy formula*** is going to keep some of you from using this technique and enjoying its benefits. I am not a psychiatrist, and it probably wouldn't help you if I were. We want to solve our problem by taking action, not talking about it.

What I hope to do is show you how to use a third step to . . .

7

Crash Through Mental Roadblocks

Shelley:

> *I regularly masturbate and even have wet dreams, but I have never had an orgasm during sex. Even though I frequently have sex with men, I am shy about asking for what I want. I enjoy the feeling of having a man inside me, but no man has taken the time to stimulate me to orgasm. Sometimes I can't wait for him to leave so I can 'finish' myself.*

Most of the women who read this book will be able to use the first two steps I've outlined here – **female-superior position and assisted masturbation** – to have quicker orgasms at their beck and call, but some may feel intimidated at the idea of masturbating themselves while their partners watch. Feeling intimated is going to negate anything else you might do to increase your sexual appetite.

You have set up your own mental roadblocks.

Up until now we have focused on the first major female sex organ for pleasure, the clitoris. The genitals are central to orgasm, but so is the brain. *The brain is the second major sex organ.*

Scientific evidence leads us to believe that the capacity for orgasm is probably universal. There is a small island in the South Pacific named Mangaia where female orgasm is considered both a male obligation and something that can be LEARNED by the young women. All Mangaian women have orgasms after brief foreplay and protracted intercourse. Male prowess is measured by the pleasure he provides his partner; in Mangaia it is essential that a good lover guarantee his partner reaches orgasm at least once before he climaxes himself. Reaching orgasm for the females gives the male partner his own pleasure and a special thrill. In this case, we can see that anatomical differences do not hinder pleasure, because all Mangaian women must learn to achieve orgasm, and do.[24]

Are American women *satisfied* with love-making without orgasm because reaching orgasm during sex is just too much trouble for her and/or for her partner? Have we compensated by denying that orgasm is important? We have waited for American men to do for us what the Mangaian men do for their partners. But with sexual expression being what it is in our culture, we have waited a long time.

In America, female sexuality, especially non-procreative sexuality, is repressed. This has helped to cause widespread inhibition and guilt and an inability of many women to reach orgasm. Even though there are many women who can enjoy sex without fear or guilt, that is probably not the norm in this country. Perhaps we still live in the shadow of the early Catholic church and Victorian repression. Even though the church never attained full acceptance of its rules and regulations, the unnatural pressure of abstinence during that time was practiced enough to produce a rich crop of mental disease.

Sexual repression causes mental disease and sexual perversions. We have evidence of this phenomenon today in the abundance of sexual abuses by *abstinent* priests.

Even though some of his theories were wide of the mark, Freud was convinced that excessive repression of sexual instincts was detrimental to the psychological well-being of the individual. According to Freud, Victorian prudery (including the idea of the passive wife who does not enjoy sexual intercourse) was a principal cause of neurosis and psychopathology of the times. In *Technology of Orgasm* by Rachel Maines, we learn that sexually repressed women were diagnosed as "hysterics." Examples of this today would be mass neurosis exhibited when innocent people were prosecuted in the alleged child porno rings in the day-care scandals of the 80s.

Repression and perversion may be the result of the same attitudes that suppress female orgasm. A sexually repressed woman feels sexual guilt, repression and shame over sexual acts like masturbation. She likely avoids pornography and shows less interest in sex than her more free-thinking counterparts. A sexually repressed woman manifests her inhibitions physiologically as well as psychologically. She is much less likely to feel aroused by erotic stimuli than are individuals who are sexually carefree.[25]

Why? Is she different physically? Most likely not. These differences occur because of standards set by parents, religion, or culture, not genetics.

Psychotherapy can lower the inhibitions and enhance the sexual pleasure of a woman who is sexually "disinterested." Your background may be keeping you from maximizing your sexual potential. This book can help. If it doesn't, and if you feel you need professional help, please get it.

Are Women Less Easily Aroused Than Men?

The presumption that men are more easily aroused than women is a long-standing myth, embraced by women, men, writers, and even scientists. It is a myth that discourages and subjugates the sexual expression of women.

In the Victorian era of the mid-to-late nineteenth century, Dr. William Acton, a noted American physician and acknowledged sexual authority, expressed the common sentiment of the day. Writing that "the majority of women (happily for them) are not very much troubled with sexual feelings of any kind,"[26] he reinforced a double standard. Women were elevated to moral superiority over men, while at the same time denied their feelings of human passion. Prostitution was considered an outlet for the "animal" lusts of men, while marriage, motherhood, and family were hailed as the one and only true pursuit of women.

Looking back, we can understand how women participated in this attitude, allowing it to flourish. Sexual intercourse was brutish and short, and birth control did not exist, causing at least some of women's reluctance to engage in intercourse. Fear of pregnancy, which was dangerous and painful, would have considerably dampened female passion.[27]

Unfortunately, women are labeled similarly today – *passionless* in the Victorian era and *less passionate* than men today. From the cradle up, we are labeled, categorized and stuffed into neat little boxes before our sexual personalities have time to emerge.

The "mystique" of the female orgasm, specifically that women take so much longer than men, comes from the past when we were considered more psychologically delicate than men, that we enjoyed sex only when in love, that our orgasms were dependent upon feelings.

Are we more enlightened today? Not necessarily. Modern research is designed to support this presupposition. Research of gender differences often analyze responses to *male oriented pornography* and to analyze the subjects' *reported* frequency of intercourse. Based on what the subjects *say about themselves*, these experiments invariably find that men are more arousable than women. Subjective reporting renders this type of research unreliable at best and at worst, inaccurate and misleading. Few people can accurately recall events from their recent past.

Since men report that they masturbate more often than women, this is commonly used to prove that men have greater sexuality. But this statistic doesn't allow for cultural bias and is not a fair measure of whether men actually *enjoy* masturbation more than women. Men are culturally conditioned to masturbate more. *Women and girls are taught that men want sex more; they grow up believing it, and act accordingly.*

Women are not slower than men to become aroused and satisfied, and their orgasmic potential is as much and possibly greater than that of males. Both Kinsey's and Hite's research reported that most women, like most men, can masturbate to orgasm in a little over four minutes, even if they don't reach orgasm during intercourse. In Kinsey's sample, 45 percent of the female masturbators reached orgasm in less than three minutes. Carol Travis and Carole Wade pointed out in 1984 that "during masturbation, especially with an electric vibrator, some women can have as many as fifty consecutive orgasms," a figure that must have raised the ancient specter of female insatiability in more than one male mind."[28]

Try it now. Close this chapter and masturbate. Time yourself with a clock. How long did it take? Most women can masturbate to orgasm in 2-4 minutes. If you do, you're AVERAGE. Now why can't you reach orgasm during sex? Simply because sexual intercourse is an extremely inefficient way to stimulate the clitoris.

In fact, women do not take longer to reach orgasm than men, and are aroused as quickly. Several lines of research have shown that if erotic stories that appeal to both men and women are used, differences in arousability disappear, both at the genital level (measurements of pelvic blood flow) or self-reported.

If you got an early start, so much the better. **Women who report having masturbated as young girls or adolescents tend to orgasm more readily during sexual relations with a partner.** Our cultural standard has played a significant role in determining orgasmic potential, but female orgasmic capacity may be learned. The bottom line is that women who can reach orgasm in four minutes while masturbating are not slower to be aroused than men. *We have been lied to, and we have lied to ourselves.*

Fulfilled at Last!

The first thing we women have to do is to stop downgrading sex and saying it is not important to us.

***Cuddling* is not a replacement for a fulfilling sexual experience.**

You either experience orgasm or you don't.

We must not accept the repression of our sexual self-interest. In accepting responsibility for our own orgasms, women are finishing the job of the sexual revolution.

More women are starting to demand orgasm, independent of whether their partner has an orgasm or not. The female orgasm is not mysterious. The entire key is adequate stimulation of the organ that nature gave you for that primary purpose. *Since most women can masturbate to orgasm in four minutes, then obviously secondary or inadequate stimulation of the clitoris has led to the misconception that women take longer than men.*

In other words, you **CAN**.

If your brain still tells you that you **CAN'T**, then maybe it's time for . . .

8

Love with the Proper Stranger

You might masturbate forever without orgasm.

But . . .

When your mind creates an image meaningful and powerful enough to negate fear, guilt, and shame, you release into that *forbidden* interior world of your own sexual psyche and you can achieve orgasm.

The brain's role in sexual pleasure cannot be overemphasized. Kissing, cuddling and fondling are not inherently pleasurable or even inherently sexual. It's our brain that makes them so.

Your mind will help you achieve orgasm faster than before. It will either inhibit your orgasm or free you.

Step Three

Step One, position, and Step Two, masturbation, are no good if used alone. What occurs in the brain is as important to sexual response as having genitals. Using our brains to make images and fantasies may be ***essential*** for most women. Why? Eyes open or eyes closed, sexual pleasure is not ***strictly dependent on anatomy***. The body parts play their role, but sexual stimulation requires interpretation and emotional elaboration of what your body feels at any given moment.

Can fantasy help you negate physical reality, ignore guilt, and overcome any inhibitions you might feel? Yes. Fantasy can help you concentrate on how your body feels, help you forget about your fight with the boss, forget the kids, how you look or any other distractions. Fantasy helps you ignore the overt experience (at least the things that distract you), and enjoy the covert one.

Your personality, learning and morals affect how, when and even *if* you fantasize. Some people fantasize all the time. For others, fantasy is a poor substitute for the real thing. For others, fantasy is **DIRTY**, even immoral.

Judy:

> *Once I started fantasizing, it came in pretty handy. I was dating a dull guy, nice enough and sex was good, but he was not a terribly exciting fellow. At the time, that was fine with me. Exciting definitely has its limitations – like unreliability – and John was nothing if not reliable. To spice things up when we made love, I would put him in a favorite fantasy. I imagined John coaxing two college students to make love to each other while he watched, and then he joins them for sex. I would never enjoy anything like that in real life, but thinking about it really turned me on. I was much more aroused by the John in my fantasy than the one in real life.*

Until recently, locker room wisdom maintained that there was no such thing as feminine lust; that women, unlike men, were incapable of separating sex from emotion, and could enjoy sex only if they were in an ongoing, emotional relationship. My experiences and the women I have interviewed and studied contradict this myth. **Many, though not all, women have fantasies that are not about husbands or lovers, but about men they will never see again, someone with whom there is no relationship.** Fantasies spice up lackluster relationships, make their partners more desirable. If they fantasize about the usual lover, they may add a characteristic that he lacks in real life.

Women use the mystery and adventure of the unknown and uncommon to enhance their sex lives.

Allison:

> *I don't like to get on top during sex. I'm five-six and 165 pounds, and I feel silly hopping up and down.*

Learning how to fantasize during sex is especially important to most women because it can help us ignore our own bodies. Women never-endingly criticize themselves. We constantly compare ourselves to swimsuit models or *Playboy* centerfolds. We imagine that our men see us as fat, that they too are comparing us to those centerfolds. Men have not learned to hate their bodies, or to be especially concerned about what their partner thinks. Prepared early in life for rejection in their sexual pursuits, they are rarely inhibited by their own bulging bellies and balding heads. You are not turned off by a less than perfect lover, are you? Not if you really like the man. Yet we are afraid that men judge us on the basis of physical perfection.

Constant worry about what our partner thinks is incredibly inhibiting to our enjoyment of the sex act.

Fantasy is a way of saying "fuck you" to our brain, "fuck you" to our partner's opinion of our bodies or our performance, to mom and dad, and to all those who went before us, who taught women that enjoyment of sex, *for sex's sake*, is wrong.

That is why fantasy is *absolutely essential* for many of us. If we are too fearful to touch between our legs, if we are too ashamed to watch ourselves in the sex act, we can close our eyes and let our minds drift to other scenes. In a perfect world, women would be confident and self-assured, totally accepting of their bodies. Failing that, by using a favorite fantasy, we can make our bodies any way we want, younger, prettier, sexier, a *Playboy* centerfold. **Anything is possible when we close our eyes.** You won't be watching your body (or his) in action unless that particularly turns you on. You don't have to try to keep your stomach sucked in, your shoulders pushed back, or your chest stuck out.

Fantasizing will help you ignore any guilt and overcome any inhibitions you might feel when you take a more aggressive role in sex. With fantasy, not only can your body be improved, you can actually be someone else. Lose yourself in fantasy like you would lose yourself in an exciting movie or a good book. A new you takes over your body – you are Scarlet O'Hara, Michelle Pfeiffer in *The Fabulous Baker Boys*, or Sharon Stone in *Basic Instinct.* It's up to you.

NO ONE WILL KNOW.

Is Fantasizing Wrong?

Sandy:

> *I never fantasize during sex. That would be unfaithful. I give Charles my full attention.*

Are thoughts or dreams more threatening to our sexual partner than what actually takes place in real life? Women appear to be more concerned about *mental faithfulness* than men. Why worry? Women do not accept the role of sex for what it is, a biological function independent of monogamy. Our closest genetic primate relatives, Chimpanzees and Bonobos, are not monogamous. Monogamy is a social contract that helps us satisfy cultural and familial needs (like the rearing of children) best fulfilled by a partnership of two. We remain faithful because we have chosen to do so. If we are thinking about someone else, so what? That doesn't make us unfaithful. Fantasies are related more to how we learned about sex than they are to our feelings about our partner.

If we were never allowed to fantasize or never allowed to *even think* of someone else, most of us would suffocate.

Men seem to know instinctively that some fantasies are not bad while others are good. Men's fantasies typically are about beautiful women, famous actresses, and models who are always sexually available. They fantasize about scandalous sex, including threesomes, public sex, orgies, and bondage, acts they have never done and have no desire for in real life. Even though they may imagine these wild scenarios, it may be the mental image of a specific body part that gets them off.

Should you feel jealous? **Develop a rich fantasy life of your own, and extend the same consideration to your partner.** Allow him to think of other women, to fantasize. If a man really loves or cares about you, he loves the whole package, not just individual body parts of the beautiful and sexy women he sees in everyday life.

Beth:

> *Do I fantasize? You bet – about any and everything. I fantasize about having two men at one time or having sex with someone else while my boyfriend watches. I fantasize about getting oral sex from under the table at a restaurant, or about being screwed during a gynecological exam. Usually I don't have time to make an elaborate fantasy during sex because I come too soon, but conjuring up any one of these quick images will do.*

The **forbidden** is a very important element in sexual fantasies. We can play out any ideas that come into our head without feeling guilt or suffering recrimination. *Fantasy improves our mental health by offering an element of excitement that we can't get and wouldn't want in real life.* Things that are harmless in fantasy have definite drawbacks in the world of reality; incest, sex with strangers, or unfaithfulness would cause a lot of grief if we indulged in real life. Fantasies aren't sick; only hurtful *behavior* is sick.

Amy:

> *When I finally learned how important fantasy was for my orgasm, I started fantasizing about anal intercourse a lot. Did that mean that was really what I wanted? Joe and I tried it during sex one night. I hated it! It was mostly uncomfortable. Yet, I still think about it when I have sex. When I fantasize about anal intercourse, it really turns me on.*

Be naughty. Fantasy works because what is forbidden is exciting.

What about women who invent elaborate fantasies of domination or maybe even rape? Theories abound about this tendency. Some think that if a woman fantasizes about being *forced*, she can invent a wild scene while remaining a *nice* girl technically. If you imagine rape scenes, that doesn't mean you want to be raped. I personally believe that most of us are lazy sometimes. Letting someone else take the lead – even in fantasy – lets us off the hook.

It may be that we tend to fantasize the *opposite* of what we are like in daily life. A friend of mine, a woman I consider rather passive in her relationships and too dependent on men, liked to fantasize about dominating or seducing younger men. Another friend is rather dominant and self-reliant. She fantasizes about being seduced or dominated by rough, hairy types. The important thing is, do not worry about real life morality. Fantasy doesn't have anything to do with what we want in real life.

Never underestimate the power and the thrill of the forbidden.

It is up to you to determine whether your fantasies of the forbidden, including immorality, rape, domination, and infidelity mean pleasure or pain, whether they are good or bad, beautiful or disgusting. Remember, we are talking about FANTASY, not real life activity.

It has long been thought that men and women are complete opposites in their sexual fantasies, that a woman's fantasies are built from previous sexual experience, created about someone she already knows in romanticized circumstances. In other words, women want romance and intimacy in their fantasies, while men emphasize physicality and the unfamiliar.

In formal interviews and casual conversations with friends, I find that is not always or even often true. Beth's fantasy (and she is not as unusual as you might think) seems anything but *romantic* to me. Erotica written by women, for women, like Nancy Friday's *My Secret Garden*, shows women having some wild fantasies that are very graphic indeed.

How to Fantasize

My own current fantasies tend to fall into two categories: brief flashes and more detailed stories. I use the brief category during masturbation and/or sex, but use the more elaborate fantasies, adding and changing all the time (like writing a story) for daydreaming. Then flashes from the longer daydreams serve as visuals during sex. I am rarely present in my own fantasy; I tend to *observe* my fantasy as if it were a movie or a book. That way I'm not emotionally involved. I don't have to suffer the tumultuous emotions that often accompany sex in real life. That is, *sex without pressure.*

Your fantasy "hero" can be a knight in shining armor, the mean, dirty member of a motorcycle gang, or the guy lying beneath you. Although I can't speak for everyone, it probably won't help if you make him too pristine or pure. I enjoy my fantasies because they are *dirty*, not because they are *romantic*. That's why they are so much fun.

However, if you prefer a romantic fantasy, by all means, go for it. If you do not fantasize already, start making up stories in your head and build on them. Fantasizing is more than physical and genital imagery, more than butts or breasts. Think in terms of daydreams. Write stories in your head with yourself as the main character, only make yourself younger, thinner, prettier, more voluptuous, or more virginal, if that helps. Start using your story when you masturbate by yourself, and finally, a favorite fantasy will help as you masturbate during the sex act itself.

You can build your stories with no intention of climaxing if you wish. But when you are masturbating alone or while engaged in intercourse, you will learn to get to the good parts of your fantasy: a hand squeezing your breast, his penis inside you, his body pinning you against a wall, so on and so on . . .

You can imagine the rest.

Erotica and Pornography

If you are having trouble concocting your story, I suggest pornography, hard or soft core, which you can find in movies, books and magazines. Hard core means you actually see the sex act itself, including ejaculation, plus penises and vaginas. Soft core means the sex is simulated. Pornographic films don't have much of a plot, and are often ineptly directed and acted, but they fulfill the true function of genuine porn which is to get us turned on.

Pornography shows us that sex is **FUN**. Maybe the plots aren't very realistic, but the actors and actresses seem to be having a great time, without guilt or shame. This fact, plus the liberal use of multiple partners, homosexual sex, anal sex, and interracial sex, constitutes "SIN" by some, but if you can free yourself from conventional notions, you can enjoy pornography too. You are not actually *doing* any of those things – you are merely watching.

It is commonly thought that men and women differ significantly in how they respond to porn and erotica. Most explicit, Triple XXX porn is targeted at a male audience, whether heterosexual or homosexual. Films, videos, and magazines portraying nudes and people engaged in various sexual activities are supposed to be the types of visual stimuli that appeal to the average man.

It is commonly assumed that men *look* and women *feel*.

Some women protest that they are not excited by explicit films. Women are thought to favor fantasy that provides an emotional context for the erotica contained therein, the softer more imaginative side. This also goes back to the misconception that our fantasies are always "romantic."

The home video market has shown women a world of sexual possibilities. Life has never been the same since the invention of the VCR. Not only can women take home films like *9½ Weeks* and *Blue Velvet* for closer scrutiny and instant replay, but X-rated films have become more explicit, available, and increasingly targeting the female market.

Lab researchers have found that women can be just as aroused as men by pornographic films, especially if the plot features a woman as the main character. Given the proper stimulus, women are aroused by visual stimulation just like men, so porno films are great for people who have trouble fantasizing. Some favorite classics are *Deep Throat, Behind the Green Door,* and *Illusions of a Lady.*

As for books, the type of pornography women prefer is largely an acquired taste, but a sleazy pornographic book works best for sharp stimulation. The level of explicitness desired is a matter for each individual, but it increases as we become more familiar with the type of material. When you are learning to masturbate, a thin paperback can be held in one hand, while giving the other hand access to genitals and other parts. You can use the stories you read or your own spin-offs for fantasies, or learn about other women's fantasies from books like Nancy Friday's *Women on Top.* Sexual fantasies are never dated. Older books like *The Story of O*, the books of Anaïs Nin and Henry Miller can still get us turned on.

Playboy, *Penthouse*, and *Playgirl* have explicit letters to the editor. Although they may seem strange, some of them are probably similar to your wildest fantasy. "True" romance or confession magazines often have good, sleazy stories.

Start using pornography to help with masturbation.

After a while you can call up these scenarios during sex; even just a small portion of one will do the trick.

I have stated explicitly that this book is about pleasing you, but many of us are going to be concerned about what our partners think. Will your lover be happy when he learns that . . .

9

It's His Turn to Be Lazy

By now you should have learned how to achieve orgasm on demand by using the ***quick and easy formula***; how to time the speed of your response by using the female superior position, the better to reach your clitoris for masturbation; and how to use fantasy (closing your eyes) to help overcome any mental roadblocks you might have. Hopefully, you are now ready to try this method. You are convinced . . . *almost.*

How Will Your Man Respond?

Do you have a vision of yourself straddling your man, "riding" him with your eyes closed, thinking about someone else or someplace else, masturbating like crazy, and he **FREAKS OUT**?

That is not going to happen. Not in 999 out of 1,000 cases. Most people think the primary male sexual problem is failure to achieve erection. Is controlling ejaculation the worst problem men face? **IT IS NOT.** ***It is failure to enjoy sex.***

In some surveys, more than *one-half* of men in ongoing relationships report dissatisfaction with sex.

This may surprise you, but it shouldn't. Today, a man finds his expertise is based on skills, foreplay, timing, and an emphasis on withholding orgasm for an indefinite period of time until he can satisfy his female friend. No wonder men are dissatisfied. In recognizing that women are entitled to experience orgasm fully, a man's climax tends to be the accomplishment of a challenge, the completion of a project rather than closeness, intimacy and FUN.

That's not to say that men don't enjoy sex. Usually they do. But their sexual encounters can be enhanced just like yours. Your man will like this technique. Just like the Men's Warehouse spokesman, **"I *guarantee* it."** Not only does it feel good, but also, men are visually oriented, and more likely than women to be aroused by the sight of a naked body or a depiction of a couple making love. He will enjoy the vision of you straddling his penis. In the female-superior position, he experiences **maximum** exposure of his penis to your vagina.

Watching you at play, freed from his usual responsibilities, most men find it easy to remain stimulated. He will see you masturbating yourself and perhaps playing with your nipples, a picture most men find highly erotic. You can invite him to do some of the stroking himself.

The female superior position also gives the man more ejaculatory control because there is less stress and tension in his body. He is more relaxed because he doesn't have to support his own weight. A 1978 *Playboy* poll found that most men feel fine about the male-inferior position and many actually prefer it.

Men tend to initiate sexual encounters, but they place great value on more assertive sex partners. They like the variety. **They appreciate the fact that they don't have to wait so long for the woman to finish; they don't have to work so hard at something that should be fun; and, even if they beat the woman to orgasm, she can still finish within a reasonable amount of time by manipulating her genitals herself.**

Bill:

> *Like most men, I fantasize about sexually aggressive women, but most of the women I knew seemed too timid about sex, confining it to a dark corner, shutting it off most of the*

time. I began to wonder if sex was something women did to please men, not themselves. I had given up hope of finding a woman who desired and appreciated sex as an enjoyable biological necessity. Finally, I met Jane. She wants sex, not simply because she loves me, but because she loves sex. For me, this is the ultimate thrill.

Fear as an Aphrodisiac

Your new sexual attitude may make your partner a little bit afraid of you. Don't worry, this can be good for your relationship. Recent research has shown that the emotion of FEAR can be a potent aphrodisiac.

In one experiment, men volunteers were each assigned a strikingly beautiful female who they were told was their research partner. At the same time they also learned that the experiment was for studying the effects of electric shock. The experimenter assured some of the men that they were in the control group so they wouldn't be shocked. The rest were told they were to receive painful jolts of electricity. After a short period, the experimenter came back and privately asked each man how attracted he felt to his beautiful "research partner." The ones who were nervously awaiting the shocks found the women a lot sexier than did those in the control group.

**We insist on safety and security.
Once we get it, we're bored.**

If your man sees you taking a new attitude toward sex, sees you seizing control of your own sexual response and suspects that you may be fantasizing about another, his fear reaction may be aroused. Your fantasies may intimidate him. You are doing things that frighten him, so he is going to be threatened. He may be awed by your new heightened sexual abilities and your display of fearlessness. You have assumed the female-superior position and actually engaged in self-stimulation, an act you previously only performed in private.

In short, he may be just a little bit afraid of you! That's good, because while your new orgasmic ability is improving YOUR sex life, his fear has intensified HIS. **Combine this with your renewed enthusiasm, and you may have the same kind of exciting, adrenaline-driven sex you had the first months of your courtship.**

David:

> *I admire Deirdre's healthy lust for attractive bodies of the opposite sex. She had slept with over 40 men when we met and has an aggressive sexual appetite. She is more knowledgeable in bed, more willing, assertive and confident because of her experience with other men. Our openness with each other has heightened our passion and intensity.*

Some men may have to unlearn their old way of doing things. For men who think that sex equals movement, and that thrusting the pelvis is an automatic response to genital contact, they will have to learn to lie still and feel. Ultimately, most men will agree that . . .

10

A Woman's Place is on Top

Modifying the Technique

There are some women who will choose to modify the ***female on top*** **PLUS** ***self-masturbation*** **PLUS** ***fantasy*** formula because of their own personal needs.

Here are several modifications you can try:

(a) When you are on top and your partner's penis is inside you, lean forward. Rest your hands or elbows on the bed or on his shoulders or chest. This position allows you to thrust your hips freely.

Move up and down, around and around, side to side, monitoring his pace. Monitor his response by watching his face, slowing down when he gets too excited. Nibble on his neck, ears, face and lips. If you can comfortably reach them, suck his nipples too.

(b) Try concentrating on twitching the inside of your vagina, as you would if you were trying to cut off urine in mid-stream. When your vaginal muscles come into play, squeezing, pushing, and pulling, this causes exquisite sensations to your lover's penis.

(c) You can try letting the man masturbate your clitoris, especially as foreplay. But many of the men and women I interviewed found that this is an awkward and uncomfortable position for his hand. It is nearly impossible for him to understand the pace and pressure you need for your most efficient orgasm. **You can do a better job yourself.** Hopefully, you've had more practice. It is better for him to use his hands fondling your breasts or buttocks.

(d) You can forego self-masturbation during sex some of the time, if you wish. By parting the lips that cover the clitoris, you can rub your body on his pelvic bone and achieve the same effect. It will just take longer and is a little more difficult to reach orgasm in this position.

(e) You can also self-masturbate while in the male superior, "spoon," and other positions, but many women find these positions awkward for self-stimulation, and reaching orgasm is more difficult. If you are embarrassed about masturbating yourself while on top, by all means try masturbating while HE is on top. He will have to lean back to give you access to your clitoris. His view of you massaging your clitoris will undoubtedly turn him on, and this is a good way to get used to the idea of masturbating yourself during sex. He will probably try to help.

(f) In the female superior position, the man can raise his pelvis for more control and/or deeper penetration. For the man who wants to thrust, try changing from female superior to male superior right before, during or immediately after your orgasm. From this position, you can roll over into the missionary position without disconnecting. **At this point, the violent thrusting of his penis can give an extreme amount of pleasure to you both.**

(g) For the truly adventurous, a favorite trick is to stay on top and perform a 180-degree turn, so that you are facing his feet. Then you lean forward, bracing yourself with your hands between his legs, and start moving your body back and forth.

From this position you can give him a real treat by massaging his testicles. You can massage your clitoris at the same time, or rub his testicles against it.

One of your adjustments may be to stop moving if he feels a premature ejaculation coming on.

One of the more important benefits of the *quick and easy formula* is that you can climax, even if he has already beaten you to orgasm. You can finish yourself while his penis is softening inside of you.

Beth:

> *One of the most satisfying orgasms I ever had was on top of a man who had already finished. He was exhausted and still, so I masturbated myself. He was still inside me, still filling me up, so the whole thing felt great.*

Don't forget to fantasize, especially with eyes closed. Even if it's just a quick image at the moment of climax, it is guaranteed to maximize your pleasure.

Double Standard

Having presented a case that your man will LOVE your new technique, let me add that sometimes, rarely, some men do not enjoy this technique. Some men find increased sexual aggressiveness (real or perceived) in a partner threatening to their conservative expectations of male dominance in sexual matters.

After her book was published, Rachel Maines had numerous speaking engagements on the subject of her book, *The Technology of Orgasm.* These talks naturally touched on the inefficiency of penile thrusting as a means of producing orgasm in women. Maines recorded her audiences' reactions. Groups consisting only of women simply laughed and asked questions. In mixed groups of men and women, the women looked uncomfortable and asked little, even though they laughed anyway. Men fell into groups who laughed or stared, "... the former ... [are] those for whom my research confirms that women are as sexual as they had always hoped, and the latter are those for whom it confirms that women are as sexual as they had always feared."

Maines discovered that some people, mostly men, took her findings personally and resented them as implied criticism. One man criticized her reasoning because using the vibrator to create orgasm was "not the real thing." One of the female audience spoke out, "Don't you see, most of the time, it's better than the real thing."[29]

A man may not want to give up the superior position because it symbolizes his desire for male dominance. This kind of man may not want you to have had sex with too many men, give sexual instructions, or be obvious about birth control (which is, of course, your responsibility in this man's eyes). Why?

The inexperienced and inept woman can't compare sexual partners and doesn't know the difference between a great lover and a poor one.

What can I tell you about this kind of man? As male superior, in control of your orgasm, he is doing nothing less than **GRANTING HIS PERMISSION** for you to be fully sexual.

The sexual revolution gave us a lot of freedom, but sometimes we are not freer people. We give away our freedoms with both hands. Many of us still find it hard to get what we want, need or like in bed.

Maines was challenged: if her thesis that women are satisfied only with direct clitoral stimulation is true, then women don't need men. Her response? **If orgasm is the only issue, men don't need women either.**

Simultaneous Orgasm: Why Not?

Some men insist on simultaneous orgasm because they (consciously or unconsciously) believe in male dominance in sex. The ability to *control* simultaneous orgasm and determining the sexual timetable can be an expression of power. Denying a dominating partner the role of leadership in the sex act tells him that you are in control of your body's sexual responses. You are no longer the passive recipient of male technique. Many women believe that it is better to fake orgasm than to challenge this belief.

Paul:

> *When Carol and I first started going out, she had only been with a couple of other men sexually. She had never experienced an orgasm before I came along. I'm a few years older than she is, and I took my time, helping her along, finally bringing her to an orgasm. Needless to say, she was thrilled.*

Maybe it's time for both women *and* men to put aside their overly romanticized versions of the sex act. Women can achieve orgasm with a less than perfect lover. We will all just have to get used to the idea – ***men too!***

Ultimately, if you are too concerned about how your man will respond to your new technique, you are reading the wrong thing. This book is about YOU, what you need, want, and can achieve in bed, not about HIM.

If you are worried about what your sexual partner thinks of your performance to the point of sacrificing your own pleasure, perhaps you should reexamine your relationship to men. Many of us were not brought up to feel free. If you are unwilling to change, if you are willing to put up with this kind of man, then buy *The Complete Woman* or any number of books that will tell you how to make HIM happy in bed.

Or better yet, seek professional help.

Toward Better Sex

It is okay to feel embarrassed or awkward at first, maybe even a little guilty. This is just the **fear of taking risks,** the granddaddy of all mental roadblocks. As young children we are often taught to do only things that allow us to feel comfortable and secure. Even today women are trained to be dependent on men. Don't let fear keep you from using this simple method to improve and control your orgasmic response.

Women's sexual response appears to improve with time and experience. The Kinsey report found that 36 percent of women in their twenties were unable to reach orgasm, but the statistic dropped to 15 percent for those in their 30s and older. Several studies done since then have found a greater capacity for orgasm among all women, possibly as a result of greater education and experience among men AND women. Still the older women as a group are more orgasmic than their younger counterparts. Is it because older women usually have sex with older men? Older men who may have enough self-control to sustain lovemaking until their partners climax? Maybe not. The statistics hold up among older verses young lesbians, which suggests that the deficiencies of men as lovers is not the determining factor. The power of knowing your own body is what's important.

It is up to modern women to challenge the accepted definition of sex as sexual activity that leads to male orgasm. Sex without male orgasm has not popularly been regarded as INTERCOURSE, but if you do not reach orgasm during coitus, it is still considered the real thing.

There is no biological basis for female passivity, no reason why your orgasm should be slower or more difficult than a man's. Men are not naturally more self-sufficient than women, their training has made them that way. They are educated for independence from the day they are born. Imagine how surprised you would feel if he depended on you to "make" him come.

Fears are mastered in any new situation by approaching and withdrawing from the frightening situation repeatedly. Scientific studies of all kinds of inhibitions show that the repeated arousal of the fear response in small controlled doses leads eventually to extinction of that fear. If you want better sex, keep trying, perhaps going a little further or doing a little more each time.

This book is written for you, but your partner will also share its benefits. Until now, male sexuality has been stifled and straight-jacketed by our culture. The ability of men to truly let go has been held back by lack of information about women's orgasms and by traditional male and female roles.

> Being told that the man is the 'do-er' (he gives her an orgasm), while the woman

> 'responds' (she must never show the man how she has an orgasm during masturbation) limited men still more.[30]

Male sexuality is only a pale shadow of what it can become.

Fear not. Your partner will appreciate your new sexual power, and your enjoyment will enhance his.

Don't worry. Keep trying. None of us did it exactly right the first time.

If you have extraordinary personal or physical problems, I urge you to seek professional help.

I don't know exactly when or how I started using the **quick and easy formula**, but I'm sure it didn't happen all at once. It was a matter of accumulating knowledge and experience, and of putting the three steps to work at different times for different reasons. The CATALYST was my essential laziness. I just knew there had to be a quicker, easier way.

Along the way, I have been able to share this knowledge with many women. Now it's yours. Sexual arousal and orgasm are not that different between men and women. By taking control of your sexual response, you no longer have to be a follower, locked into the supporting role. Remember, sex without YOUR orgasm is not sex either. It is your **RIGHT** to enjoy sex on an equal basis with men.

Angela:

> *After being married for 9 years, having most of my orgasms only by self-pleasuring in secret because having them during sex took too long, I finally increased my rate of coital orgasm from fifty percent to 100 percent. My husband and I don't have to give up before I've come because we are exhausted. I don't have to fake it to get the sex act over with. I finally decided that the woman's place is on top. By masturbating myself, closing my eyes and fantasizing, I have found 'Old Faithful' in terms of having reliable orgasms in a matter of only a few minutes. That way, if we take longer, it's because it is fun, not because we have to.*

Most of us are victims of patterns and expectations that were set long before our time, but it is up to us whether we continue to be victims or take control of what is rightfully ours. We know how to have orgasms during masturbation. A man controls his orgasm by thrusting his penis against the vaginal wall in a way that maximizes his sexual satisfaction, and it's not considered selfish, infantile, or sick. How strange that women haven't learned to use their masturbating knowledge and skills in our sex with men.

Jonathan:

> *I no longer have to thrust like a madman for 30 minutes or two hours so Cheryl can climax during sex. Thrusting all night made me feel like a machine, and I didn't like it. I felt alone, and it stopped being fun. Now I enjoy being on bottom when she stimulates herself. We both reach orgasm easily, free of any pressure to 'perform' for the other's benefit.*

Gary:

> *I love and encourage my wife's stimulating herself to orgasm while we have sex. After 15 years of marriage, she finally feels free to express herself without embarrassment. I'm happy knowing she can have an orgasm anytime she wants, and I love watching her face in the throes of pleasure. It's awe-inspiring to watch a woman who enjoys sex as much as I do.*

Creating orgasm for yourself can be beautiful, deeply and lovingly shared. Removing the tension of not having an orgasm, the agony of a prolonged, uncomfortable sexual encounter, dislodging the dishonesty of a faked response, and creating equality of responsibility in the sex act can deepen the respect you have for your lover, improve communication and strengthen the love and commitment you feel for each other as a couple.

The clitoris loves power, and it strives to reinforce the sensation of playing commando. The anthropologist Helen Fisher has found that women who are easily and multiply orgasmic have one trait in common: they take responsibility for their pleasure. They don't depend on the skillfulness or mind-reading abilities of their lovers to get what they want. They know which positions and angles work best for them, and they negotiate said postures verbally or kinesthetically. Moreover, the positions that offer many women the greatest satisfaction are those that give them some control over the sexual choreography: on top, for example, or side by side.[31]

Cherish Your Sexuality.

No other woman is like you. The sounds you make during sex, the feel of your skin, the passion in your eyes, and your facial expression when you reach orgasm are unique to you and valued by any man who really loves you. Ever heard a man describe why Michelle Pfeiffer, Demi Moore, Sandra Bullock and Meg Ryan are considered most attractive among thousands of more beautiful faces? The most common word used is that they "glow." Learn to value yourself and you will become more radiant and exciting.

Learn the ***quick and easy formula***, and it will be easy.

Sexually fulfilled and content,
that same luminous glow will be yours.

Appendix

References

Abramson, Paul R., Pinkerton, Steven D. (1995). *With Pleasure: Thoughts of the Nature of Human Sexuality*. New York: Oxford University Press

Angier, Natalie (1999). *Woman, An Intimate Geography*, New York: Mifflin Company)

Diamond, Harvey and Marilyn, (1985). *Fit For Life*, New York: Warner Books, Inc.

Diamond, Harvey and Marilyn, (1987). *Fit for Life II: Living Health*, New York: Warner Books, Inc.

Fisher, S. (1973). *The Female Orgasm*, New York: Basic Books

Foucault, M. (1990). *The History of Sexuality*. New York: Vintage

Freud, S. (1938). *The Basic Writings of Sigmund Freud*. New York: The Modern Library

Friday, Nancy (1991). *Women On Top: How Real Life Has Changed Women's Sexual Fantasies*. New York: Pocket Books

Heiman, J. (1976). *Becoming Orgasmic: A Sexual Growth Program for Women*. Englewood Cliffs, N.J.: Prentice-Hall

Hite, Shere (1976). *The Hite Report on Female Sexuality*. New York: Macmillan

Hite, Shere (1981). *The Hite Report on Male Sexuality*. New York: Ballentine Books

Kinsey, Alfred Charles (1953). *Sexual Behavior in the Human Female*. Philadelphia: Saunders

Maines, Rachel P. (1999). *The Technology of Orgasm: "Hysteria," the Vibrator, and Women's Sexual Satisfaction*. Baltimore & London: The Johns Hopkins University Press

Masters, William H. (1966). *Human Sexual Response*. Boston: Little, Brown)

Tiger, L. (1992). *The Pursuit of Pleasure*. Boston: Little, Brown & Company

Web Sites

www.erotica-readers.com

www.sexuaity.about.com

www.jpspublishing.com

Index

Notes

1.Natalie Angier, *Woman, An Intimate Geography* (New York: Houghton Mifflin Company, 1999)

2.Paul R. Abramson, Steven D. Pinkerton, *With Pleasure: Thoughts of the Nature of Human Sexuality* (New York: Oxford University Press, 1995)

3.Abramson, Pinkerton, *With Pleasure*, 7

4.*The Female Friend; or the Duties of Christian Virgins to which is added, Advice to a Young Married Lady.* By F L Esq. (Baltimore: Henry S. Keating, 1809), 48

5.Ferdinand Lundberg, and Marynia F. Farnham, New York: Harper & Brothers, 1947, 275

6. Virginia E. Johnson and William H. Masters reported in their book *Heterosexuality* (Harper-Collins, 1994) that as many as 70% of women don't have orgasms through intercourse alone.

7.Rachel P. Maines, *The Technology of Orgasm: "Hysteria," the Vibrator, and Women's Sexual Satisfaction* (Baltimore & London: The Johns Hopkins University Press, 1999) quoting Diane Grosskopf, *Sex and the Married Woman* (New York: Simon and Schuster, 1983) 35-43

8.Maines, *The Technology of Orgasm*

9.Angier, *Woman, An Intimate Geography*, 58

10.Woman, *An Intimate Geography*

11.Edward W. Eichel, *The Perfect Fit: How to Achieve Mutual Fulfillment and Monogamous Passion Through the New Intercourse* (Signet 1993)

12.Maines, *The Technology of Orgasm*, 62

13.Angier, *Woman, An Intimate Geography*, 69

14.Hite, Shere, *The Hite Report on Male Sexuality* (New York: Ballentine Books, 1981), 426-427

15.Hite, *The Hite Report on Male Sexuality*, 426, 429, 435

16.Hite, *The Hite Report on Male Sexuality*, 733

17.Rachel Maines in *The Technology of Orgasm* quoting Frank S. Caprio, *The Adequate Male* (New York: Medical Research Press, 1952), 70.

18.Hite, Shere, *The Hite Report on Male Sexuality*, 721

19. The definitive books on this subject are the *Fit for Life* books (I and II) by Harvey and Marilyn Diamond. *Fit for Life* shows the reader how it is just as important to be as clean on the inside as it is on the outside, maybe more so. The deal with the subject of Toxicity more thoroughly than most books, and the books are pure pleasure to read. See, *Fit for Life* (1985) and *Fit for Life II: Living Health* (1987) by Harvey and Marilyn Diamond(New York: Warner Books, Inc.)

20.*The Technology of Orgasm*, .p. 89

21.Maines, *The Technology of Orgasm*, 19-20

22.Maines, *The Technology of Orgasm*

23.Nancy Friday, *Women On Top: How Real Life Has Changed Women's Sexual Fantasies* (New York: Pocket Books, 1991), p. 25

24.Paul R. Abramson, Steven D. Pinkerton, *With Pleasure: Thoughts of the Nature of Human Sexuality* (New York: Oxford University Press, 1995)

25.Abramson, Pinkerton, *With Pleasure*

26.Abramson, Pinkerton, *With Pleasure*, 121

27.Abramson, Pinkerton, *With Pleasure*

28.Maines, *The Technology of Orgasm*, 48-49

29.Maines, *The Technology of Orgasm*, xiii

30.Hite, *The Hite Report on Male Sexuality*, xiii

31.Angier, *Woman, An Intimate Geography*, 70